# The complete book of
# SCRAPBOOKING

bay books

# CONTENTS

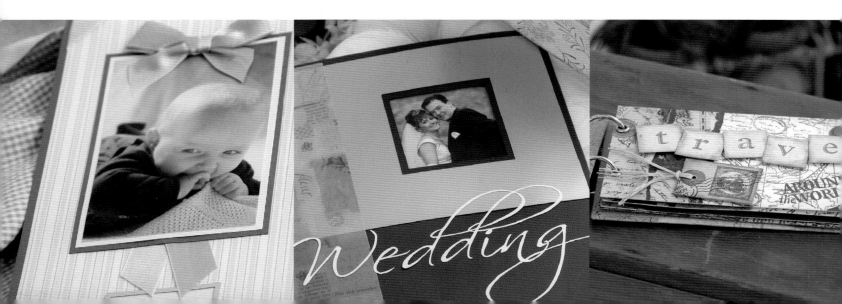

# INTRODUCING
# SCRAPBOOKING

Modern scrapbooking is a rapidly growing craft geared at teaching the preservation of photographs and capturing life's significant moments through words or 'journalling'. The art of scrapbooking combines the principles of photograph preservation with the principles behind the design of an appealing layout.

## HISTORY

Scrapbooking began several hundred years ago, when people used diaries, journals and handmade albums to record thoughts, recipes, poetry and quotes. The earliest surviving book dates from the seventeenth century in Germany.

Throughout history, artists and other creative thinkers have kept scrapbooks of drawings, ideas and text. Among them was the great Renaissance artist and scientist, Leonardo da Vinci. Amazingly, many of his pages have been the inspiration for today's printed papers, vellum and rubber stamps.

References to 'common-place books' appear as early as the 1590s. These books included collections of diary entries, drawings and newspaper clippings.

Even Shakespeare's play *Hamlet* mentions the recording of notes in a commonplace book. In 1706, the British philosopher John Locke published

his *New Method of Making Commonplace Books*, which advises readers on the best way to preserve ideas, proverbs, speeches and other notes. By 1825, the term 'scrapboook' was in use and a magazine devoted to the hobby, *The Scrapbook*, was in circulation.

In the late nineteenth century, scrapbooks attained popular status and many magazines published ideas on what to include in them. Mementos, such as newspaper clippings, pressed flowers, calling cards, letters, ribbons and locks of hair, all found their way into personal scrapbooks. Pictures were etched or engraved onto the pages.

During the Victorian era, even more embellishments were added to scrapbook pages, such as ornamental vignettes and cut-outs. Die-cuts (pre-cut paper shapes) and stamps were introduced in the 1870s and companies manufactured images specifically for inclusion in these albums.

In the late nineteenth century, the invention of the camera added a new dimension to the art of scrapbooking. As photography became more widespread and affordable, photographs began to appear in scrapbook albums.

During the 1880s, an increased focus on the study of genealogy–the identification and preservation of family roots–gave scrapbooking another new direction. This fascination continues today as many families research their genealogies as a means of discovering connections to the past and preserving the family heritage for the future.

Today's scrapbooks may vary greatly from those of the 1500s. The manner in which they are presented and preserved has evolved, reflecting the knowledge of preservation and archival techniques. However, one common thread connects the past to the present–scrapbooks have always told a story.

## SCRAPBOOK OCCASIONS

Many scrapbookers begin with a particular event in mind: a baby is born, or someone in the family is getting married, starting school, having a significant birthday, graduating, retiring or experiencing hard times, such as the death of a loved one. Once a goal or reason has been established, it is time to sort through photographs and memorabilia, organizing them and then ordering them to tell a story.

The great thing about scrapbooking is that anyone can do it. The only prerequisites are being able to cut and paste. This craft appeals to all age groups. Children love to get involved and a section of this book is devoted to kids scrapbooking for themselves.

The creation of a scrapbook can bring families together as they share highlights and rekindle memories. Children enjoy looking through family scrapbooks,

especially when events meaningful to them are scrapbooked and journalled.

Scrapbooking the difficult or sad times, like divorce, death, moving, or any major change in the family structure, can even help children and adults. The pages of the scrapbook, with patterns made from colours, shapes and textures, emphasize that life is an imperfect but dynamic mixture of events and emotions.

A scrapbook can be created for any theme: a year album, baby album, heritage album or school album. Albums can also display an individual's collections, such as cars, teacups, teddy bears, quilts, letters or postcards.

Many businesses, from florists to restaurants, use scrapbooks to showcase their products and services.

Albums can be created as special gifts, such as mini brag (baby) books, kitchen tea (recipe) collections, wedding anniversary and birthday books.

The beauty of this craft is that there is no right or wrong. Scrapbooking should be a meaningful experience for the creator, free from judgment or critique.

The selection of photographs, papers, embellishments and journalling should reflect the scrapbooker's own personality and their taste.

Modern scrapbooking is a communal pastime. Scrapbooking shops often support groups of scrapbookers by providing access to shop equipment. Scrapbookers derive the practical benefit of sharing costly equipment, such as punches and tools, as well as finding inspiration and mutual interests. It's also a great way to make new friends.

The ideas and techniques shared in this book will provide the beginner or experienced scrapbooker with the inspiration and knowledge to create a wonderful album, filled with mementos for the family and future generations.

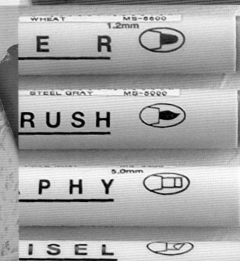

# CONSERVATION AND STORAGE

Scrapbooking is all about preserving memories for generations still to come. Scientific knowledge regarding the conservation of paper, photographs and other materials has given the modern scrapbooker a distinct advantage. This craft now provides a safe, archival means of storing and displaying treasured photographs.

## DETERIORATION

In recent decades, attempts to store and display photographs have unwittingly led to their destruction. Magnetic albums or albums with plastic coverings made from polyvinyl chloride (PVC) were used to keep precious photographs safe. Unfortunately, the materials in these albums contained chemicals that, with time, break down to form acids. These acids, in turn, begin breaking down any adjacent papers or photographs. The scientific term for this is acid migration.

Many papers contain lignin, a chemical compound derived from plant matter. In time, lignin will also break down causing the paper to yellow and become brittle. The process of deterioration affects surrounding material such as the paper and any photographs with which it is in contact.

## REMOVING PHOTOGRAPHS FROM OLD MAGNETIC ALBUMS

Keen scrapbookers will want to take measures to salvage photographic material from old magnetic albums.

The process for removing photographs is simple, but requires some care. A blow-dryer should be held about 12 cm (5 inches) away from the album. The heat from the blow-dryer will help to soften the glue.

Dental floss can then be used behind the photographs to lift them without damage to these treasures. If this does not work, an acid-free product called Un-Du can be used. Simply put a few drops into the scoop and apply carefully underneath each photograph. The photographs should lift easily without any ensuing damage.

## CONSERVATION TERMS

**Acid** The chemical property of a material with a pH level less than 7.0

**Acid free** The make-up or chemistry of materials that have a pH level of 7.0 or higher

**Archival quality** A description of materials that are permanent, durable or chemically stable, and are suitable for preservation

**Lignin** A compound found in paper derived from plant matter. It is the part of the plant that gives it strength and rigidity

## RESTORATION

Once photographs are removed from old albums a quick inspection will reveal if there has been any damage caused by the PVC covers and acids.

Replicate any photos that are in danger of deterioration. This can be done by scanning or reprinting photos or even making colour photocopies on acid-free paper as a temporary solution.

Damaged photographs can be restored in many different ways. Professional photo labs provide restoration services for photographs and negatives.

Extremely old photographs and photographic plates should be assessed by specialist restorers.

## SCANNING

Photographs can also be scanned at home on a quality scanner. The scanned image can then be manipulated using a photo software package. Images of photographs scanned at home can be saved onto a floppy disk or CD-ROM as a JPEG or TIFF file, then taken to a professional lab for developing. This will avoid wear and tear on a printer.

A new generation of scanners has recently emerged and these will automatically restore damaged photos as they are being scanned.

Technology has placed the tools that were once limited to a few specialists in the hands of every scrapbooker. The section on Using Computers will feature many more ideas that will help build a knowledge base for today's scrapbooker.

## NEGATIVE STORAGE

Negatives and slide film should always be stored away from photographs. It is suggested that negatives be placed in polyester or polypropylene plastic sleeves to ensure that they will be free from any damage caused by acid migration.

Not all negative sleeves provided by photo developers are acid free, so take a little time to organize their storage.

Once negatives are stored properly, they will last for years, allowing scrapbookers to reprint photographs that may be decades old.

Professional photo labs are constantly upgrading their services. Quality, old negatives can actually be reprinted with better colour saturation and brightness than in their original printing.

# YOUR PHOTOGRAPHS

Photography is the key element of modern scrapbooking. The ordering and labelling of photographs form the scrapbook's story. Organizing photograph collections, rather than saving them for a rainy day that never arrives, is essential. After all, who wouldn't appreciate having a well-prepared photo album from generations ago?

## PHOTO DATING TIPS

It can be difficult to sort photographs into years as many people do not record this information on the back of photographs. However, these factors will help make it easier to identify the year or approximate date in which a photograph was taken.

- Age of the people
- Fashion
- Furniture
- Cars
- Hair styles
- Travel, holidays
- Homes lived in
- Schools attended

## SORTING

The best way to start organizing years of photographs is to first move all the photographs, albums and memorabilia to one location in your home. Once a comfortable spot (that doesn't need to be cleared at dinner time) has been established, you can sort through the photographs. The easiest way to sort is in chronological order, working backwards from today.

Clear off a large work area and grab some stick-on notes to label each year. As photos are being sorted they can be placed into the corresponding year group. Once this is completed the next step is to revisit each pile and re-sort the photographs into months or events.

## LABELLING

Unfortunately, too many people have collections of old photographs in their homes that have been passed down through the generations without any identifying details. Often, these details are lost forever as the people who may remember names, dates and locations are no longer living.

As the sorting process is taking place, record any information related to the photographs to ensure that all relevant information is captured, such as who is in the photo, when was it taken, and its location. The sorting process often rekindles memories and feelings associated with the past, so make the most of any reminiscences by recording them.

Use a soft graphite pencil to write on the back of photographs. Do not use a ball-point pen or lead pencil as they can damage the photographs.

## CHRONOLOGICAL ORDER

A set of photos labelled and sorted into chronological order is the starting point for a scrapbooker's collection.

Simply record the year on the front of each box then place the photographs in order.

If there are several photos of the same event, in lieu of writing on the back of each one, use a journalling card to record all the information relating to that event. Once the recording is complete, place the card in the box in front of the photographs.

Journalling cards make scrapbooking a particular event easier as they provide all the details at a quick glance.

## THEMES

As photographs are being sorted into chronological order, themes will begin to emerge. This is a great place for the novice scrapbooker to start. Decide on a particular theme and then gather photos. This theme could be a recent holiday, house renovation or family celebration.

As a beginner, it is advisable to save wedding, baby or heritage photos for scrapbooking at a later time as these are the most precious photographic resources. The results should reflect the care and creativity that your heirlooms deserve.

Scrapbooking skills will improve with knowledge and experience. This book will provide the appropriate techniques to develop your skills and to scrapbook valued photographs with confidence.

## PHOTO STORAGE

Photo boxes are an ideal storage solution when sorting photographs into chronological order. However, make sure the photo boxes are made from acid-free cardboard.

Take the time to add in the journalling cards as it will save time and energy when planning the layouts.

Store the photo boxes in a cool, dry location to avoid any damage from light or mould.

# MATERIALS AND EQUIPMENT

When you are first assembling your scrapbooking materials you will start with the most basic cutting and pasting tools, but the scope of the craft is so wide that a fantastic range of materials and equipment can be utilized in the creation of each page. Specialist products are available from scrapbooking stores.

### PAPER

All paper used for scrapbooking should be acid and lignin free. Cardstock is a thick, sturdy paper that can be used to hold all the elements of a page together. Printed paper tends to be thinner. Photographs are either directly mounted (attached) onto cardstock or matted (adhered to layers of paper) first, then mounted. Cardstock is available in more than 400 colours and numerous textures. Printed papers also come in a wide variety, including hearts, animal prints, floral, lace, water, checks and stripes.

As current scrapbooking trends have originated in the USA all sizes for scrapbooking are in inches. The most common paper size is 12 x 12 inches or 30.5 x 30.5 cm. Other sizes are available, such as 8 1/2 x 11 inches or 21.5 x 27 cm, but selections in patterned papers are somewhat limited.

### ADHESIVES

Any adhesive used in a scrapbook must be acid free. Some adhesives allow for items to be shifted, others set quickly.

Options include glue dots, bottled glue, glue sticks, liquid glue pens and silicone glue. Photo tape has a peel-off backing and double-sided tape comes on a tape roller. Adhesive photo corners are useful.

A good choice for a novice scrapbooker is the double-sided tabs that come in a box or dispenser. The advantage is that they are refillable and cost effective.

Glue sticks are great for children, due to ease of use and reasonable pricing.

The choice of adhesives also depends on what is being attached, its size and weight. Fabric is best attached with an acid-free craft glue (PVA). Silicone glue is great for tiny items but heavy items such as pockets or foam core require strong glues.

### PENS

A pen or marker used in a scrapbook must be of archival quality, waterproof, fade resistant, non-bleeding and acid free.

Pens used in scrapbooking are made from pigment ink; therefore the ink is permanent. When starting, a good-quality black pen with a monoline nib is essential for journalling.

There are several varieties of pens available. These include monoline, calligraphy or chisel point, brush, scroll, and gel pens. There is also a red-eye pen that is used for removing the red from peoples' eyes in photos.

The Vanishing Ink Pen is filled with special ink that will vanish off the pages within 24–72 hours. It is a great alternative to the lead pencil as it will not leave any stray marks. The full range of pens will be discussed in the Using Pens section of this book.

## CUTTING TOOLS

Scissors are used extensively in scrapbooking so purchasing a sturdy, sharp pair of paper scissors will prove to be a valuable investment.

Every scrapbooker should also invest in a paper trimmer. A 30. 5 cm (12-inch) paper trimmer is recommended as it will provide a sufficient cutting surface for an entire sheet of the standard 30.5 cm (12-inch) square cardstock. There are many different brands on the market today. The most versatile paper trimmers have an extension ruler and a few different types of blades for scoring and for perforating.

Fancy scissors are often used to create different edges. They can be purchased in a wide variety of styles.

Cutting systems have also been developed to help in cutting shapes like circles and ovals. Many of them can cut a variety of shapes as well as letters of the alphabet.

## PAGE PROTECTORS

It is important to place completed pages directly into a page protector to prevent people touching and damaging the material. Once people see the completed pages they will be eager to look through them over and over again. Keeping pages protected will ensure that photographs and papers will be free from fingerprints and dust as well as acids from handling.

It is important that page protectors be made from polypropylene, polyethylene and polyester plastics. Always avoid any products made from PVC as they will be harmful to photographs.

Events featured in scrapbooks often require more than a double-page spread, so expanding page protectors are a suitable option. These will also allow for more memorabilia to be included in the layouts.

Special pocket pages are available for featuring and protecting memorabilia.

## TYPES OF ALBUMS

The most popular album size is 30.5 x 30.5 cm (12 x 12 inches), but smaller sizes are also available. There are three main types of albums: three ringed, strap-hinged and post-bound.

Three-ringed binders are easy to use, hold more pages and are often cheaper than other types of albums. Completed pages are inserted into page protectors that can be easily moved.

Strap-hinged albums allow the book to expand to the length of the strap. Facing pages lie flat, enabling continuity in a double-page spread. The albums usually come with a white background page. Page protectors for these albums can be side-loading or top-loading.

Post-bound albums are expandable, with the addition of extra posts. Pages in post-bound albums can be easily moved around and arranged. Page protectors for these albums are top-loading.

# SEVEN STEPS TO COMPLETING A PAGE

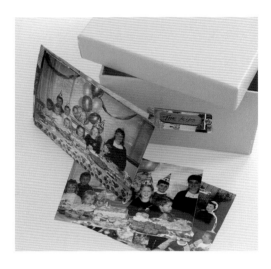

### 1 SELECT A THEME

Select a group of photographs that go well together and clearly tell a story. The number depends on the size of the photographs and the theme. A single large photograph on a page is effective in special scrapbooks, such as a wedding or heritage album.

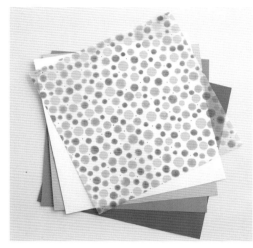

### 2 CO-ORDINATE PAPERS

Take the photographs with you when purchasing papers as there are more than 400 colours of cardstock and thousands of printed paper designs to choose from. Select different colours and place them behind the photographs to see which combinations work best.

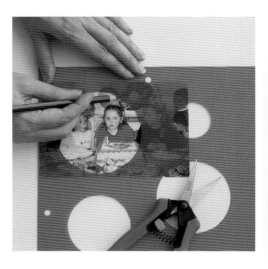

### 3 CROP PHOTOGRAPHS

Cropping is where some of the photographs are trimmed and cut. Scrapbookers can try inventive or minimal cropping, depending on the quality of the photographs and individual taste. However, do not crop precious or one-of-a-kind photographs.

### 4 MAT PHOTOGRAPHS

Matting is the piece of cardstock adhered behind the photographs in order to highlight them. The number of layers and the colour choices can vary, depending on the desired impact. Refer to the section on Matting for more information.

### 5 LAY OUT THE PAGE

Once matted, lay the photographs out on a two-page spread of cardstock. Re-arrange the items on the page until the desired balanced design has been achieved, then attach the items to the page. Refer to the section on Design Principles for more information.

### 6 CREATE THE TITLES AND JOURNALLING

Decide on a title or heading and then see how it will be displayed in the available space. The journalling or stories about the layout are very important. Try to record all those details that future generations will find interesting.

# 7 ADD MEMORABILIA OR EMBELLISHMENTS

Last, add any memorabilia that may be relevant to the pictures. If there is no memorabilia, consider adding some type of embellishment that will enhance and complete the layout.

# DESIGN PRINCIPLES

Scrapbooking applies the design principles used by photographers and graphic artists. You can easily achieve an effective layout after spending some time practising these basic rules. Individual creativity is the extra ingredient that will make each design your own.

## BASIC LAYOUTS

Before beginning the actual page layout process, ask the following questions: What is the goal or theme of this layout? Who is the layout for? What feelings should this layout evoke? The next step is to determine the focal point. In scrapbooking the focal point is usually a photograph; however, it can also be a journalling item, piece of memorabilia, or an embellishment that emphasizes the theme of a page. Since the focal point is the first place the eye catches, proper placement is critical. Often a photograph can be enlarged or cropped to achieve emphasis. Matting is another effective way to establish a photo as a focal point. Double or triple matting a photograph will naturally draw attention. Framing will also draw the eye to the focal point.

## BALANCE

The first rule of creating a great layout is achieving balance. In a balanced layout all the elements are arranged so that the entire layout has a consistent visual weight. If a layout is unbalanced it will cause the visual flow to be affected, diminishing the value of some photos. Artists often turn their canvases upside down to check for balance. This technique actually works well for the scrapbooker. It will direct the eye to the unbalanced portion, which can often be easily corrected by a slight adjustment or addition. Embellishments such as charms or die-cuts, could provide the necessary element for balance.

## RULE OF THIRDS AND 'Z' MOVEMENT

The rule of thirds is a technique that has been used by artists and photographers for decades. Applied correctly, it can help to achieve an effective layout with visual appeal. Usually applied to rectangular pages it works just as well on the standard 30.5 x 30.5 cm (12 x 12 inch) page. The rule divides the page into thirds both horizontally and vertically, creating nine smaller sections and four points of intersection. Placement of the most important elements on the intersections will create a visually effective layout.

Creating a 'Z' movement on a page is another great technique. This is achieved by arranging elements so that they form a 'Z'. This guides the eye naturally through the page from left to right, then down, creating an appealing flow.

## SHAPES

Geometric shapes are visually appealing and add flair to any layout. While cropping a photograph can add shape and interest, extensive cropping is not recommended.

Cutting a sharp corner with a circle can soften a feature but still provide emphasis. Devices such as punches and decorative scissors provide a quick method of shaping elements on a page.

Embellishments can also quickly add shape to a layout. They include circular, rectangular and square tags, stickers, metals, buttons and charms.

## COLOUR

Colour is the predominant element in a page design. It has the ability to dictate the entire mood. Colours are categorized as either warm or cool. Purples, blues, and greens inspire feelings of tranquillity and peace. The warm colours—reds, yellows and oranges—evoke energy and playfulness. The depth of colours can also affect the tone of a layout. Deep, dark colours suggest a regal atmosphere while light, pale colours imply a delicate, soft feel. Earthy tones are appealing as the colours are neutral and do not compete with other tones in the photos.

Colours in a layout should either complement or enhance the focal point in the photo grouping. There are a few colour schemes that can be followed. The monochromatic scheme uses one colour selection in different shades. A complementary colour scheme uses colours that are found on the opposite sides of a colour wheel. The triadic colour scheme selects three colours of the same value. This means they must be all soft, bold, muted, light or dark. Finally, the split complementary colour scheme utilizes one colour from the photo and one or more complementary colours. Experiment with these schemes, duplicating a few good photos so that layout options can then be compared.

Less is more with colours. Try a limit of three colour choices with a ratio of 60 per cent dominant colour, 30 per cent complementary colour and 10 per cent additional complementary colour.

# BACKGROUNDS

Create backgrounds for your scrapbooking page by selecting a piece of cardstock or printed paper that co-ordinates with your photographs. You will find the easiest way to make an appropriate choice of paper is to have your photographs with you to get a good match. The most difficult procedure is choosing from the amazing variety of papers that are available.

## PATTERNED PAPER TIPS

Try these ideas for using patterned paper backgrounds to enhance your design.

**Creating a border**  Cut or tear a strip of patterned paper for a quick border accent.

**Matting photos**  Photographs can be emphasized with a double or triple mat. The patterned paper can appear as the second layer. Using cardstock against the photograph separates it visually from the patterned paper and further distinguishes it as the focus of the page.

**Creating leading lines**  Cut patterned paper into strips and place them horizontally, vertically or diagonally across the page to direct the eye to a focal point.

**Creating embellishments**  Cut out decorative elements from the sheet of patterned paper to provide interest, balance or extend a theme.

## USING PATTERNED PAPER

Patterned paper can potentially add personality to a scrapbook page. It can reflect the theme or nature of an event. The whole piece can either be used as the entire background or cut into smaller pieces to make a more complex background for the page.

## INSPIRATION FROM PHOTOGRAPHS

Backgrounds for a page can also be created by utilizing elements within the photographs. Themes from photographs can be extended into the background as well. This may be as easy as selecting a paper that matches or re-creating an element from the photographs in the background. When re-creating an element from the photos look for something small, such as a pattern from an item of clothing, or an architectural element.

If a piece of printed paper cannot be found to enhance or complement the photos, consider designing one using the techniques discussed in Part Two of this book, such as Rubber Stamping.

## COLOUR BLOCKING

The colour-blocking technique is actually what the name suggests. It involves arranging two or more block shaped (square or rectangle) pieces of paper of complementary colours to build a geometrically patterned background. Colour blocking is a quick way to add impact to a page (refer to the layout entitled My First Set of Wheels).

Colour-blocked pages are simple to create and often do not require additional accents–just some favourite photos. Experiment with colour blocking and try varying the size and number of blocked areas. Practise using different colour combinations, but make sure your colours support rather than detract from the photographs. Colour-blocking templates make this technique even easier. Simply use the template to indicate where the colour-blocked pieces should be placed.

Venice

# CROPPING

Cropping is the cutting or trimming of photos to achieve a desired shape, size or effect. Photographs are cropped to highlight the focal point and remove any unnecessary details including those that do not enhance or relate to the overall theme. Cropping equipment ranges from scissors and a pencil to elaborate cutting systems.

## WHEN NOT TO CROP

Before you start to crop, consider that limited cropping is often more effective than a busy layout that has too many trimmed shapes. Sometimes framing can be a more suitable option to highlight the focal point.

Never crop one-of-a-kind photographs. If negatives of the photographs are not available, do not crop them.

Do not crop Polaroid photographs. The liquid inside is poisonous and if the photographs have not set properly this liquid will destroy other photographs.

## CROPPING TECHNIQUES

Beginners are advised to start with the simplest cropping methods. A paper trimmer is best for cutting straight lines. A template and removable grease pencil (a 'chinagraph' or wax pencil) is good for cutting circles and ovals.

Cutting systems, such as the Coluzzle nested template system, will also cut shapes. However, some cutting systems may take a little getting used to. Since everyone has some bad photographs in their collection, it is recommended that these be used for practice.

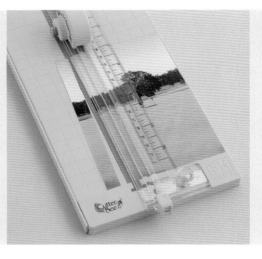

1 The decision to crop a photo must first take into account which photo will be the focal point of the layout. Select the shape and size for cropping, remembering to leave details in the background. Line up the square shapes under the paper trimmer. Trim the photograph vertically and horizontally.

2 Simple templates can be used for cropping curved and irregular shapes, as well as rectangles. Place the template over the selected part of the photo and draw around the shape with a grease pencil. Cut the shape out with a sharp pair of scissors. Rub off any bits of grease pencil left behind with a soft cotton cloth.

3 To use the Coluzzle nested template system, place the photograph on the special backing provided. Position the Coluzzle template over the photo and select the best size for cropping. Cut along the guidelines with the Coluzzle cutter and snip the section remaining on each side with a pair of sharp scissors.

## SPECIAL PUNCHES

A square punch is a quick and easy way to crop out sections of a photograph.

There is a wide range of sizes to choose from. Every scrapbooker should have at least a few different large punches in their collection.

Oval and circle punches are great for cutting those difficult curved lines.

Punches that are designed to crop the corners of photographs are another useful investment for scrapbookers.

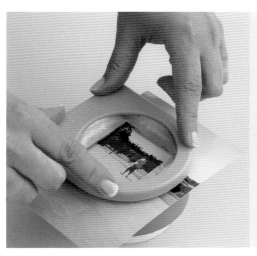

1 Line the photo up on the wrong side of the square punch.

2 Place your hand on the punch and apply even pressure.

# MATTING

Matting is the process of cutting and placing complementary paper singly or in layers behind a photograph to highlight it. As well as being decorative, matting with acid-free cardstock ensures that photographs are separated from other items on the page.

### CREATING A FOCAL POINT

The matting beneath a photograph needs to be carefully selected so that it does not take the focus away from the photograph. Plain cardstock is the easiest way to achieve highlighting without detracting from the photograph. However, when layering with several mats, printed paper can be used effectively. Try papers that echo colours, patterns or themes in the photo.

Since matting draws attention to the photographs, several layers can be used to create a focal point.

### MATTING RECTANGULAR PHOTOGRAPHS

If the photograph is a square or rectangle, adhere it to the corner of the cardstock. Use the markings on the paper trimmer to place the photo and cut the remaining sides at the same distance.

It is not necessary to cut the entire piece of paper. You need only cut to the end of the photo. This saves paper and allows for the matting of other photographs in varying sizes.

If matting more than one colour, repeat this process for each layer.

### MATTING CURVED PHOTOGRAPHS

Photographs can be cut into curved shapes by using oval and circle templates and special equipment such as the Coluzzle nested template system. If a cutting system has been used, try selecting the next size up to cut the layers of matting.

An easy-to-use tool called Magic Matter is also great for matting curved photographs. Use it to draw an evenly distanced line around the photo, then cut along the line with a pair of scissors.

1 Select pieces of coloured cardstock which match colours in the photograph. When using several layers of matting, make sure the colours work well with each other.

2 Glue the photo to the corner of a piece of cardstock. Use a paper trimmer to line up and cut the matting. Build up the other layers in this way, measuring the size increases with a ruler or paper trimmer.

3 Try varying the widths of the matting to add variety. Tearing the edges of the matting (refer to the section on Paper Tearing) will also add interest. When the layers are complete, adhere the matted photo to the layout.

## MATTING TIPS

Cut out the matting with a pair of fancy scissors to create variety.

Using a combination of colours is a great way to highlight photographs.

Varying the width of the matting can produce an interesting visual effect, especially when creating a focal point.

Embellishments, such as eyelets, can also be used on the matting to further draw the eye to the featured photo.

As with cropping, less is sometimes more. There is no need to triple-mat every photo on a layout.

An alternate pattern, such as single, then double, matting can be used to create interest on the page.

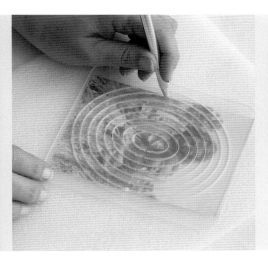

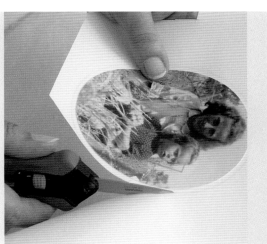

1 Use a template (such as the Coluzzle nested template system) to cut the photograph into an oval shape. The matting can then be cut at the next size up on the template, or cut manually using the Magic Matter system.

2 To use the Magic Matter system glue the oval photograph to the cardstock. Select a Magic Matter disk—the size will determine the width of the matting. Mark the cutting line by moving the Magic Matter disk around the photograph with a graphite pencil.

3 Cut out the matting and rub out any pencil marks with an eraser or a piece of clean cloth. Additional layers of matting of varying widths can be created with the different sizes of Magic Matter disks.

# JOURNALLING

Journalling is the creation of titles, headings and text on the scrapbook page. It is one of the most important aspects of modern scrapbooking. It records important facts, dates and recollections that might otherwise be forgotten. Journalling also tells the wonderful stories behind the pictures–it allows a scrapbook to come to life!

## JOURNALLING TIPS

An easy way to remember the kind of information to include in scrapbooks is to think of the five **W**s:

**W**ho is in the pictures? Record the first and last names, especially of the people who are not part of the immediate family.

**W**hat was happening?

**W**hen did it happen? Always include the date somewhere on your page.

**W**here did it happen? Include as much detail as possible such as addresses, restaurants, signs, buildings and landmarks

**W**hy did it happen? Explain the whole story.

## THE ART OF JOURNALLING

Photographs can capture and record many memories, but those memories are not complete without words.

Journalling is really about what you would like to say if you were talking someone through your photo album. People tend to explain the story behind photographs. Scrapbook journalling needs to do the same. Of course journalling may just provide facts and dates, but it can also set the tone or scene for an album.

Journalling styles can be humorous, sentimental, informative or highly personal–or all of the above!

The decision about what to write in a scrapbook depends heavily on the type of album being created, its audience and the personality of the scrapbooker.

## RECORDING THE PAST

To help the process of recalling details, jot down notes on a personal calendar or a notepad. Journalling cards for photo boxes are a great way to stay organized. If writing on the back of photographs, always use a graphite pencil or a removable stick-on note.

When journalling for a scrapbook it is recommended that a separate sheet of paper be used, which is cut and mounted on the layout. This will prevent any costly mistakes.

Do not fret over the quality of your handwriting! The content is actually more meaningful than the appearance of the letters. Handwriting carries the characteristics of an individual's personality, making its preservation very special. Even if the computer is used for text within an album, every effort should be made to include some samples of handwriting.

## JOURNALLING THE FAMILY

When journalling, it is interesting to gather input from the people present in the photographs. Getting family members involved will make the reading much more fun and more precious in years to come. Remember to incorporate the handwriting of other family members.

Writing fond sentiments about friends and family in a journal entry is a great way to capture feelings and thoughts that will live on. As albums are revisited over time, the reading of journal entries will build and strengthen relationships.

Occasionally, people find themselves at a particular event with no camera to capture the notable moments. When there are no photographs for a particular event, it can still be successfully scrapbooked through journalling or by using other memorabilia. This will allow a record to be kept of an occasion that, in time, might otherwise be forgotten.

## HIDDEN JOURNALLING

Occasionally the journalling included in a layout is of a personal or sensitive nature and is not intended for everyone's viewing. In these cases, consider applying some hidden journalling techniques.

Journalling can be placed in envelopes or flaps that are attached to a layout.

A journalling entry can also be tucked behind photographs or other embellishments on a page.

Other more elaborate options include putting the journalling on pull-out tags, a mini-book or even a CD.

Hidden journalling can also be attached to the back of a layout, keeping its contents secure.

## JOURNALLING THE HARD TIMES

Journalling the difficult times in life will help sort out thoughts and emotions related to the event. In many cases recording them can help family members in the healing process.

Events like death, illness, divorce, natural disasters, fires, floods and cyclones should not be avoided in a scrapbook. Their presence will emphasize that life is not perfect, but rather a mixture of events and emotions all responsible for moulding a family's dynamics.

# MEMORABILIA

Memorabilia is a record of items worth remembering. It can be anything that provides information on or permanent evidence of a past event. To scrapbookers memorabilia can be just as important as photographs. Highly effective layouts can be created simply with journalling and pieces of memorabilia.

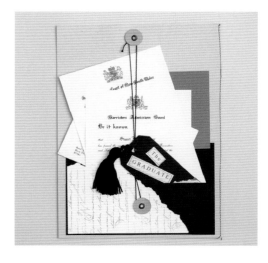

## MEMORABILIA TIPS

Following are some suggestions for memorabilia to keep:

**Babies:** ultrasound photos, hospital bracelets, baby booties, corner of a favourite blanket, swatch of fabric from the christening dress, lock of hair, first rattle, first bib

**Vacations:** maps, travel brochures, business cards, menus, postcards, hotel stationery, ticket stubs, foreign coins and notes, receipts, stamps

**Home:** cards and letters, paint swatches, house plans, old keys

**Family favourites:** handkerchiefs, charm bracelets, buttons, tie clips, hair clips, pocket watches, brooches, doilies, rings

**Records and awards:** certificates, ribbons, scout badges, ID cards, report cards, medals, diplomas.

## WHAT TO KEEP

Use memorabilia to tell a story, just as you would use a photograph. Journalling can describe the details as well as the feelings associated with scrapbooked memorabilia.

Childhood memorabilia will be treasured in years to come. Cards, letters, paintings, projects and stories from school can be scrapbooked and journalled. If the original artwork is fragile, photograph it and scrapbook the photograph. Items such as the first missing tooth, or handprints that depict a child at a particular age of development will be especially meaningful.

When photographs are not available for a particular event, memorabilia, along with journalling, can still form a dynamic layout. Knowledge of this should help free every scrapbooker from any limitations when it comes to creating a layout for any occasion or theme.

## MEMORABILIA PRESERVATION

When using original paper items, such as certificates or letters, be sure to de-acidify them with a de-acidifying spray (available from craft stores) prior to including them on a layout. These sprays, such as 'Archival Mist', contain an alkaline buffer that will neutralize any acid that is present in the paper.

Newspaper articles should be photocopied onto acid-free, lignin-free paper. They can also be sprayed with a de-acidifying spray and laminated.

Most fabrics are safe in your scrapbooks since natural fibres do not contain acid.

The Xyron laminating and sticker-making machine can protect organic items like flowers. The laminate is acid free and see through. However, do not laminate any items that may have a future use. Do not use ultrasound photos with a heated laminating machine.

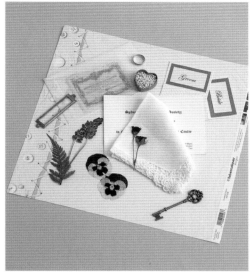

## STORING ORIGINALS

Another effective alternative is to first scan items and then reprint them onto acid-free, lignin-free paper.

If the items are especially valuable, consider scrapbooking colour copies and storing the originals in acid-free envelopes. Remember to store them in a safe place, free from humidity or direct sunlight.

Occasionally scrapbookers come across items that would be meaningful in a scrapbook but are too bulky or large for a layout. The alternative is to photograph each item. Then the photographs can easily be incorporated onto a scrapbook page and provide a permanent record in the event that the item is lost or no longer available in the future.

Items like furniture, cars, paintings and quilts can often be damaged, passed on, or sold in years to come so this will keep their place in a family's history.

## MEMORABILIA KEEPERS

Memorabilia should be removable from a scrapbook page just in case it is required at some time in the future.

Self-adhesive photograph corners enable quick removal of memorabilia and look effective on a scrapbook layout.

Another option is plastic memorabilia holders. They have an adhesive backing that can stick onto a page in seconds. They also have a flap that can be opened and closed for easy access. Memorabilia holders come in variety of sizes and are great for hair clippings, sand, jewellery, tiny shells, pressed flowers and small coins.

Clear plastic page protectors with pockets for memorabilia, such as coin collector pages, are available in different shapes. These are great for storing thin 3-D memorabilia such as coins, jewellery and dried flowers and memorabilia that is double-sided.

## POCKETS AND FRAMES

Pocket pages are useful for storing larger items of memorabilia. They can be created by the scrapbooker in any shape or style and designed to complement and enhance the theme of a layout.

Vellum is especially useful for pocket pages because it is translucent and allows the item to be seen.

Acid-free, double-sided tape is the best adhesive for pocket pages. Pockets can also be attached with eyelets or brads or sewn with fabric and thread for an impressive presentation.

Raised frames, such as box frames, also make attractive memorabilia keepers on the scrapbook page.

# EMBELLISHMENTS

Embellishments are all the extras used on a scrapbook page, such as stickers, pressed flowers or haberdashery. Embellishments accent the photographs, add visual interest or texture and can help balance the layout. Scrapbook embellishment also provides craftspeople with the opportunity to showcase their different skills.

## EMBELLISHMENT TIPS

The following is a list of embellishments available in good scrapbook stores:

- Eyelets
- Brads
- Threads
- Ribbon
- Lace
- Buttons
- Wire
- Magic Mesh
- Stickers
- Conchos
- Frames
- Fabric
- Beads
- Tags
- Paper clips
- Charms

- Slide mounts
- Page pebbles
- Metal letters
- Metal words
- Metal charms
- Pressed flowers
- Washers
- Watch parts
- Keys
- Metal photo corners
- Metal engraved plates
- Metal rings
- Jump rings
- Woven labels

## EMBELLISHING THE PAGE

Embellishments may include stickers, die-cuts, preserved plants, fabric, haberdashery and even small items of hardware. The list is extensive and often reflects the newest trends.

The great thing about scrapbooking is that it gives people with skills in a wide range of crafts the opportunity to display them. Skills such as paper quilling or sewing can be used for embellishing the scrapbook page in a unique and personal way.

Page embellishments can be either strong or subtle. First decide how the embellishment will function. For example, embellishments such as fabric, felt, mulberry and handmade paper will add a tactile aspect to any layout.

Embellishments should reflect the subject matter, so look for links between your photos and different embellishments.

## PLACEMENT

If adding embellishments as an accent, experiment with their placement.

Do not limit accents to just filling in an empty space. Place them so they are peeking out from behind photographs, use them to embellish journalling blocks, or cut off an edge to give a more natural, pleasing result.

Use groupings to bring logic to accents; for example, although leaves may look fine randomly scattered throughout a layout, they may actually be more effective if grouped in clusters of three, especially when emphasizing a focal point or journalling block.

# A walk in time

It was quite common back in the 1940's to have your photo taken while you were walking down the street.

This photo of Gwen & John Holthouse, and John's sisters Kathleen & Mabel was taken as they walked down George Street, Sydney.

# ORGANIZING TIME

Organization is the key to getting more scrapbooking done. Many scrapbookers find their craft soon becomes addictive and are keen to maximize their scrapbooking time. With a little self-discipline, forward planning and some specialist storage systems, you're well on your way to to becoming an organized scrapbooker.

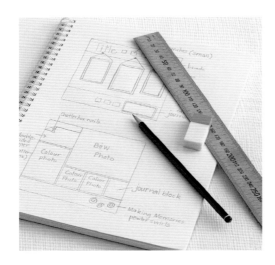  

### TIME-SAVING STRATEGIES

When you begin scrapbooking keep your equipment to a minimum so it is readily accessible and transportable.

Shop for just three or four scrapbooking layouts at a time. This will help keep you focused and on task! Visiting a scrapbook store can be overwhelming because of the large amount of products available. Purchasing too many items at once makes it easy to become lost in all the choices—and too hard to get started. Keep a theme in mind to help make the visit purposeful, allowing more time for actual scrapbooking.

Remember that each page does not need to be a masterpiece and take hours to complete. Less photo cropping and page embellishment will allow you to complete your pages more quickly.

### PUTTING IT ON PAPER

Sketch books are a great reference, especially since life is so busy and things can easily be forgotten.

Purchase a sketch book and store it among scrapbooking materials. Use it to quickly sketch layouts found in books or magazines that capture your interest. Include a list of products and embellishments or add a quick description of usable photographs. The sketches can be revisited and updated to reflect variations based on theme or personality.

A sketch book will save time because all the planning for a layout is basically completed. It can also be used as a diary to record quotes, journalling ideas, references to page numbers in magazines and memorable expressions uttered by children or other family members.

### STORAGE SYSTEMS

Keep all photographs and supplies organized and in the one spot. Store the photographs in photo boxes so they are well protected and easily accessible.

Once a layout has been sketched, purchase the required items and keep them all together in a 'work-in-progress' folder. This folder is then ready to go immediately.

Colour co-ordinate scraps of paper, then store them in an expanding file so they are easy to find when needed.

An organized tote bag on wheels will provide convenient transportation of materials.

Finally, a pared-down collection of basic tools will be light enough to transport and relocate. It makes the prospect of scrapbooking less daunting and you will find it easier to get started.

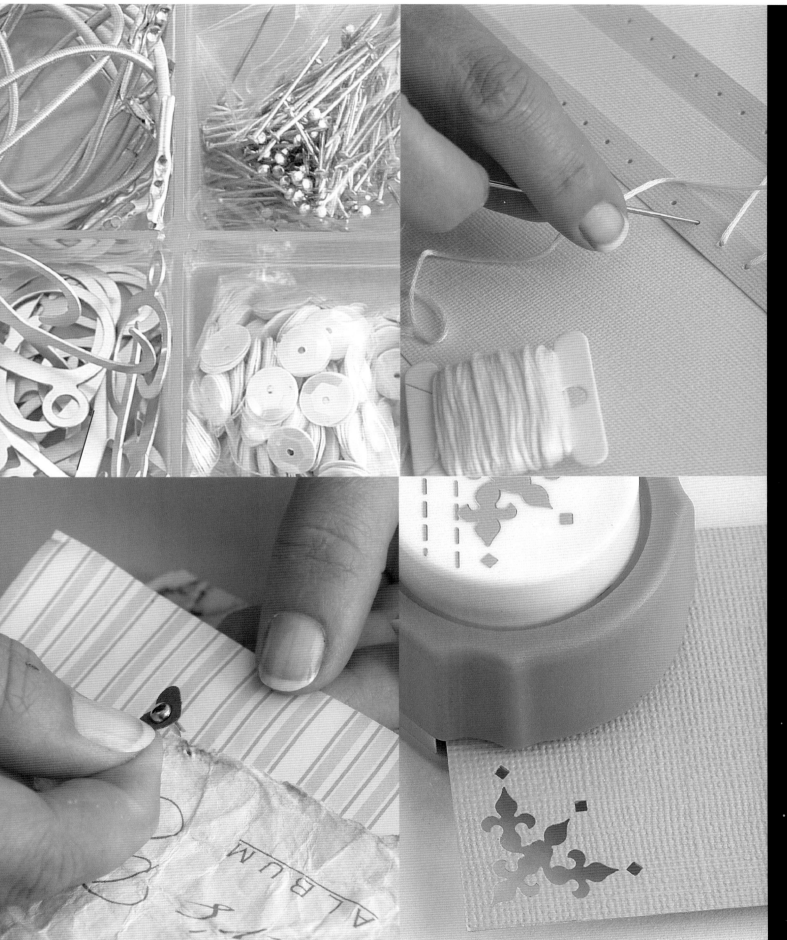

# USING STICKERS

Stickers are a quick and easy way to embellish a scrapbook layout. They are available in thousands of themes, styles and colours, including very useful alphabet and numeral stickers. With some creativity, stickers can be decorated and positioned so that they add life and movement to the scrapbook page.

## STICKER TIPS

Any leftover stickers can be used to create birthday cards, invitations and gift tags.

Try mixing alphabet sticker fonts to create a whimsical look on a layout.

Customize your stickers to reflect the overall style of the layout. Experiment with sanding and dimensional magic.

Use tweezers to help position stickers with ease.

## WORKING WITH STICKERS

All stickers used in an album must be acid and lignin free. If not, the acid in the stickers will migrate to the surrounding papers and photographs. Check for 'acid-free' on the label when you purchase stickers.

When working with stickers, try to group them together to create a scene. Anchoring stickers will create interest and depth in a layout. They must have purpose and meaning on the page so they can enhance the theme. Remember to always keep a layout balanced. This includes the positioning of stickers.

If using only one sticker on a sheet, cut around the sticker and experiment with its position before attaching it to the layout. This will ensure a pleasing result in the end.

## CUSTOMIZING STICKERS

Raising stickers will enhance realism and create a three-dimensional look. This can be done with Magic Mount, a type of three-dimensional adhesive. The layout entitled A Day at the Zoo demonstrates this technique. The stickers appear to be jumping off the page, giving them a whimsical feel.

Stickers can be customized by applying other techniques such as tearing and chalking.

If some of the stickers on a sheet are not used they will still make fabulous embellishments for other papercraft projects such as cards and bookmarks.

## ALPHABET STICKERS

When using alphabet stickers there is a sure-fire method for getting them straight, centred and in the correct position on a layout.

Simply use the top edge of the sticker sheet, placing approximately one-third of each letter on the top and allowing the remainder to hang off.

Once the word or phrase has been spelt out and spaced, take the sheet to the layout and attach the letters in the predetermined location. Peel the sheet away from the bottom third of the letters and stick this portion down.

If a sticker is accidentally placed in the wrong spot or does not work in the overall appearance of the layout, use a bottle of Un-Du to remove it.

1 Always select acid-free stickers. Check their positioning on the layout. Cut off narrow strips of Magic Mount (try 2.5 cm or 1 inch wide) with a sharp pair of scissors.

2 Cut off small sections from the strip of Magic Mount and arrange them on the sticky side (back) of the sticker. Add enough pieces so all parts of the sticker, such as the giraffe's neck, will be supported when raised.

3 Sprinkle talcum powder over the sticker to nullify the stickiness of the sticker back. When complete, peel off the backing to expose the adhesive side of the Magic Mount. Attach the sticker to your layout.

# SPECIALTY PAPERS

Specialty papers are those that do not fall under the heading of cardstock or patterned paper. Some of the most prized specialty papers include mulberry, handmade and metallic varieties. They come in a wide array of textures and thicknesses and lend extra interest or add special effects to the pages without greatly increasing the bulk.

## MULBERRY AND OTHER SPECIALTY PAPERS

Some of the more common specialty papers are handmade, metallic and mulberry. Vellum is another specialty paper used extensively in scrapbooking; this paper is covered in more detail on page 38.

Mulberry is actually a thin, fibrous paper made from the inner bark of the mulberry tree. It is pliable and loosely woven with long fibres. Mulberry paper is often torn to reveal an uneven edge, giving it a soft 'fuzzy' appearance.

There are many other varieties of specialty papers for scrapbooking, including cork, rippled cardboard, maruyama (thin mesh-like Japanese paper), suede and printable canvas. Always ensure the papers are acid and lignin free before using them in an archival album.

## HANDMADE PAPERS

Handmade papers add a wonderful texture and homemade feel to a layout. They come in a variety of colours, patterns and thicknesses.

Some handmade papers are made with leaves and flowers embedded in the fibres for a pretty touch, and some are embossed with patterns.

Handmade papers can be easily made by using leftover scraps of cardstock; paper-making kits are available at most craft stores.

## METALLIC PAPERS

Papers that give the appearance of metal in a variety of finishes, such as flat, diamond dust, mirror, pearlescent and iridescent, are known as metallic papers.

Colours range from pastels to silver, gold and black. They are often used as photo mats or cut into smaller pieces for faux-metal embellishments such as photo corners.

Inkjet printers and normal inks will not work well on this paper, so if writing on them, use a quick-drying pen such as a Slick Writer.

1 To create a torn-edge effect on matting made from mulberry paper, use a water pen, cotton bud or small paintbrush dipped in water. Draw a line of water along the paper where it is to be torn. This will help to control the tearing.

2 Gently pull the mulberry paper at the wet edges and the fibres will separate easily.

3 Allow the mulberry paper to dry completely before adhering the mat to your layout.

# USING VELLUM

Vellum is a translucent paper similar to, but thicker than, tracing paper. It is acid and lignin free and comes in a variety of colours, printed patterns and textures. Vellum provides many entrancing options for scrapbookers such as subtley patterned backgrounds, delicately layered matting, gorgeous embellishments and translucent pockets.

### CHOOSING VELLUM

Vellum takes its name from the medieval paper it resembles that was made from animal skin. Modern vellums are made from plant products and come in a range of colours, patterns and textures.

Select your vellum in conjunction with the background cardstock. Deeper or brighter-coloured backgrounds can be used, as placing the vellum on top will soften or mute the colour dramatically.

If you wish to match the cardstock to a photograph, a layer of white vellum on top will mute the cardstock, providing a closer match to the photograph.

Vellum is the ideal choice for making delicate pockets on your scrapbook pages. The translucent quality of the vellum lends elegance to the page while still providing practical storage for memorabilia.

### JOURNALLING WITH VELLUM

Vellum can make your journalling easier. In the back of this book you have been given templates for writing fonts. Simply place vellum over the top and trace with your archivally safe pen, then add colour.

Vellum can even be used with a computer printer to great effect. With some printers it helps to use a colour other than black, such as grey, brown or blue, to eliminate the bleeding process.

Print out headings or text on a sheet of paper (A4). This will show exactly where the text will be printed.

Use a removable adhesive to attach a scrap piece of vellum on top of the writing, then refeed the paper through the printer. This is an attractive, economical method for using up scrap pieces of vellum. See the Using Computers section for more ideas.

### ATTACHING VELLUM

Vellum is translucent so most adhesives will show through. However, different techniques can be used to avoid this problem.

If using vellum to mat photographs, start attaching the layers from the top. Any adhesive can be used underneath the photograph without being noticed.

If nothing is being placed on top of the vellum, there are several suitable adhesive products. These include clear-mounting tabs, double-sided tapes and vellum adhesive sprays. The least noticeable is the vellum adhesive spray, which allows the flexibility of repositioning. Access to a Xyron machine provides a big advantage as this machine can transform a piece of vellum into a sticker.

Scrapbook stores also carry a large range of brads, eyelets, snaps, paper nails and conchos that are effective when mounting vellum onto cardstock.

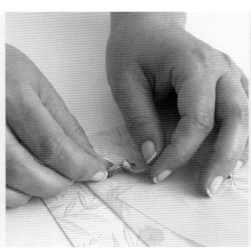

1 Cut out two rectangles of vellum to to make a pocket for your layout. Fold each piece in half then make a flap by folding at an angle as shown. The second piece should have a larger flap. Slot the two pieces together.

2 Punch three sets of two small holes into the vellum with a hole punch and hammer.

3 Secure the vellum with two pieces of matching ribbon. Thread each ribbon through the holes and tie it in a knot. Embellish the pocket as desired.

# CUTTING

Cutting techniques are an essential part of scrapbook creation. Cutting creates the shapes and titles that are integral to the layout's design. Cutting equipment ranges from a humble pair of paper scissors to the deckle-edge or fancy varieties. Precut push-out shapes are also available, as well as sophisticated die-cutting machinery.

  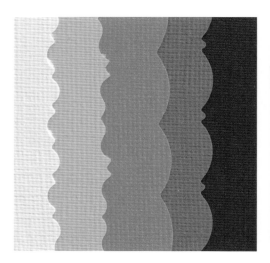

### USING DIE-CUT SHAPES

Die-cut shapes can be quick and effective embellishments for a layout. They can be layered with other colours to give them dimension or chalked to make them appear more realistic.

Die-cut shapes serve several useful functions. They can be used for journalling and for adding dates, locations, and names.

Die-cuts can hide personal journalling that is not meant for everyone's viewing.

Die-cuts can also create interesting backgrounds for a layout.

Scrapbook stores sell manufactured die-cuts that come in a large assortment of themes and phrases. They can be easily personalized and adapted to the style and colours of your layouts. Embellishment techniques (featured in the picture) include decorating with chalks, rubber stamps, printed papers and sequins.

### DIE-CUTTING MACHINES

Scrapbook stores often provide access to expensive die-cutting machines. These machines can cut through cardstock, foam, fabric, printed paper or photographs. It is recommended that no more than four layers be cut at one time, less when using heavier cardstock.

Die-cut letters can create a quick and easy title or heading for any layout. Letters can be aged or softened with chalks or highlighted with gel pens. A shadow effect can be easily created by cutting out the same letter in two different colours. The letters can then be overlapped, allowing the bottom colour to show through. Experiment with revealing the bottom letter on the bottom right or left or top right or left. Stick the letters together, then apply them to the layout.

Try to use leftover scraps for cutting out letters to minimize waste.

### SCISSORS

Fancy scissors can be purchased in a range of styles. Use fancy scissors to add flair to photograph matting or journalling blocks. When matting a photograph, try to vary the overall look by layering a fancy edge in between two straight-edged mats.

When cutting a square or rectangular shape with fancy scissors it is important to cut the mat slightly larger (about one extra centimetre or $^1/4$ inch) than required. Turn the paper over and draw lines with a ruler and pencil about 4 mm ($^1/8$ inch) from the edge. Use this line as a cutting guide. The longest points on the scissors' blade should always land on the edge of the line. This will help to maintain the correct shape.

This technique also works when you are cutting circles or ovals. Use a template on the reverse side of the paper to draw guidelines, then begin cutting.

One man all by himself is nothing.
Two people who
**belong together**
make a world. ~Hans Margolius

Teresa & John

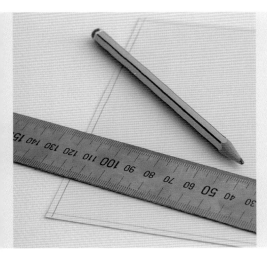

1 Cut the paper for the photo mat slightly larger (about one extra centimetre or ¹/4 inch) than required. Turn the paper over and draw lines with a ruler and pencil no more than 4 mm (¹/8 inch) from the edge.

2 Using the pencil line as a guide, begin cutting with the deckle-edged scissors. The tip of the furthest point should touch the line. Continue cutting all the sides in the same manner.

3 Turn the photo mat over. To make a more decorative edging, use chalks to highlight the deckled edges. Glue the mat to the photo.

# PAPER TEARING AND CRUMPLING

Tearing or ripping paper instead of cutting it with scissors can add definition, texture or softness to a page, depending on its application. Paper crumpling, also known as scrunching or wrinkling, is another great way to achieve a textured look without making the layout too 'lumpy'.

## TEARING TIPS

Some other popular effects achieved by using torn paper are:

Natural elements such as water, dirt, sand, trees and leaves, grass, mountains and the sky

Teddy bears, cats, dogs (anything that has fur)

Woollen items or things that are fuzzy

Flowers

## TEARING PAPER

Paper is made from compressed fibres, and tearing it breaks those fibres apart. Each type of paper will offer different effects when torn and some papers are easier to tear than others.

Straight edges can sometimes create a harsh impression that detracts from the overall appearance of layout designs. This is especially true when overlapping two or more layers of paper. Tearing the graduated edges will soften the look by removing harsh lines and corners. The eye is immediately directed to the focus, which is usually the photograph.

Many papers have a white reverse side. After tearing the paper in two, one piece will reveal a white edge while the other piece will show none. Torn pieces that reveal a white edge will provide extra definition on a page. For a softer look, tear paper dyed through and through to reveal a less stark contrast.

## TEARING TECHNIQUES

The tearing process is simple; hold one side of the paper still, and use the other hand to slowly tear toward the body.

At first, tearing might be made easier by drawing a light guideline with a pencil on the reverse side of the paper. However, tearing looks great when it has a free-flowing effect and it is not necessarily confined to the boundaries of a line. Paper looks even more effective when it is torn in a jagged, uneven or sloping line.

If tearing small pieces, use a small, controlled tearing motion. For larger pieces, tear in one smooth movement. Experiment with tearing effects on different types of papers.

Journalling boxes, page titles and photos can look effective with torn edges. However, use copies of photos rather than tearing the originals.

## PAPER CRUMPLING

Paper crumpling adds texture to the page without being too prominent. Combining the same papers on a layout —but with one crumpled and one left plain—can create an interesting background without the addition of new colours.

Crumpling paper is very easy. It can be done in two ways: dry crumpling and wet crumpling.

For the dry method, just crumple the paper by hand and then unfold and smooth it out. To obtain more wrinkles, repeat the process until the desired effect is achieved.

For wet crumpling, follow the easy step-by-step instructions. This method works best with cardstock, as most patterned papers will disintegrate when wet.

One Sunday

In     the     Park

1 Hold the cardstock under gentle running water until wet, or use a spray bottle filled with water to spray the cardstock until it is completely damp.

2 Crumple the cardstock into a ball with your hands. Carefully open your hands to see the creases made and repeat the crumpling if desired. If a small hole should appear, don't worry–this will add to the shabby look.

3 For a rumpled, uneven look, leave the paper to dry naturally. To achieve a flat but still wrinkled effect iron the cardstock while wet or dry, setting the steam option to 'off'. The end result will resemble handmade paper.

# PAPER ROLLING AND SCRAPING

Paper rolling adds yet another interesting dimension to the edges of torn paper and is especially effective when applied to photograph mats and title boxes. Paper rolling is great for producing the 'shabby' or 'worn' look often used in heritage layouts. Paper-scraping techniques will also help to achieve an aged appearance.

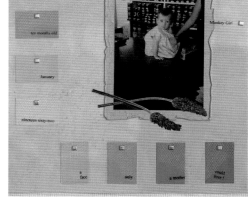

## PAPER ROLLING

Paper rolling refers to the rolling of a torn edge of paper between the fingertips until it holds itself in a rolled or curled position.

Rolled sections of paper can vary in size and tightness of roll; there are no specific rules on how the roll should look.

Different types of paper will give slightly different effects, but the best papers to use are cardstock or printed paper. Vellum and most other specialty or handmade papers do not roll well.

Space cuts along the paper's edge at uneven intervals, and make sure they do not extend too far into the paper, about 1 cm ($^1$/4 inch). The deeper the cut, the wider the rolled edge.

Some practice may be needed at first to get the rolling action just right. Too much rolling may tear or pill the paper, and too little may cause it to unravel.

## ROLLING IDEAS

Once a level of confidence is reached in this technique there are many options for its use.

Tear a hole in the middle of a piece of paper and roll the edges from the inside towards the outside, then place a photo or journalling box behind the paper so it 'peeks' through the hole.

Layer several pieces of rolled paper on top of each other and space them slightly apart so each rolled edge can be seen. Try a beach theme layout with several different shades of blue cardstock to create the effect of waves.

Roll the edges of photo mats and sit the photo inside the rolls. Roll one or more edges of journalling boxes or titles.

Colour or gild the reverse side of the paper before rolling it, so the rolled edges will be a contrasting colour and the rolling technique is accentuated.

## PAPER SCRAPING

Paper scraping will only work with cardstock, as paper is not thick enough.

The best method for scraping paper is to hold a piece of cardstock in one hand, with the edges lying straight out in front of you, so the cardstock is horizontal to the floor.

Using one of the blades on a pair of sharp scissors, scrape down the edge of the cardstock, starting at the point furthest away from you and bringing the scissors toward you.

Repeat this over and over until the cardstock starts to become a little 'fluffy' at the edges.

Wipe off the fluff and the result should be similar to the edges of the pages of an old book.

This process is also known as 'knocking' the edges and works very well with vintage-style layouts.

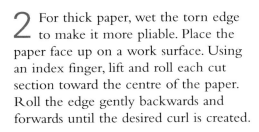

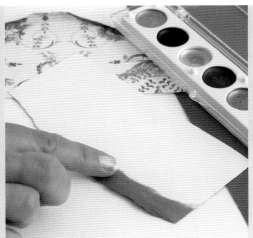

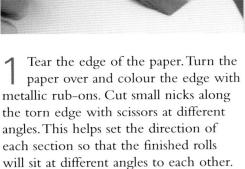

1 Tear the edge of the paper. Turn the paper over and colour the edge with metallic rub-ons. Cut small nicks along the torn edge with scissors at different angles. This helps set the direction of each section so that the finished rolls will sit at different angles to each other.

2 For thick paper, wet the torn edge to make it more pliable. Place the paper face up on a work surface. Using an index finger, lift and roll each cut section toward the centre of the paper. Roll the edge gently backwards and forwards until the desired curl is created.

3 Roll one edge on each of several large pieces of paper and overlap to create an interesting background for the page. Colour with metallic rub-ons or chalks to further accentuate the rolling technique.

# PUNCHING

Punches are versatile, easy to use and come in hundreds of different shapes and styles. On layouts, punched shapes can be used to create embellishments, interesting backgrounds and photo corners. Punched images can also be combined to create eye-catching decorations with minimal effort.

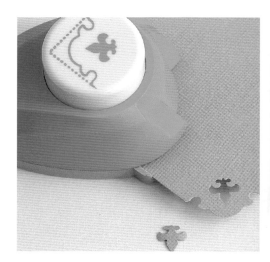

### PUNCHED SHAPES

Punches can be purchased in varying sizes of one particular shape. The most popular shape is the square punch with the circle coming in a close second. These punches can be used to create borders, headings and embellishments. They are also used to crop photos.

Other punches on the market will create decorative corners. The most basic one rolls the edges, others punch out a more elegant design.

A hole punch and hammer are essential for punching small round holes for eyelets (refer to the Using Vellum and Using Metals sections for more details).

Punching is a resourceful way to use up any scrap paper. Whole layouts can be punched with very little paper. Use printed as well as solid papers for punching projects. The printed papers add interest and a new dimension to punched projects.

### PUNCHED PATTERNS

Both the punched-out shapes and the holes they leave behind have a decorative potential; (see the 'Alfred Buckley' layout overleaf).

The possibilities of punched shapes are further increased by cutting them in half, either across or diagonally.

The shape produced by the square punch is often cut diagonally to form a right triangle. This can, for example, become the basis of a quilting pattern.

Punched shapes can be put together to form a pattern such as the attractive fleur-de-lis punched shapes that form the bridal flower motifs (pictured) in 'The Bride' layout.

Punched shapes can also be chalked, highlighted with pens or mounted, using Magic Mount for a three-dimensional effect. Extra touches include gilding, sequins and diamantés.

### PUNCHING TECHNIQUES

The easiest way to punch is to turn the punch over, slide a piece of paper into the punch and press down with the heel of the hand.

A Punch Mate can be used to complete projects that require a lot of punching. It has a lever that minimizes the effort needed to punch a shape.

Since punches are a precision cutting tool they require some care to maximize their lifespan. They may be used on 80 gsm to 230 gsm (3 oz to 8 oz) paper, depending on the type of punch.

Manufacturers do not recommend that punches be used on light paper or uneven cardstock as they could cause the punch to jam.

Store punches in a dry environment to prevent corrosion. If a punch becomes corroded, a dab of light oil should remove it. Remember to remove any excess oil before reusing the punch.

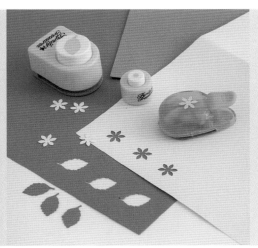

1 Use green paper for punching out the leaf shapes. Slide the green paper into the punch and press down. Repeat this, working along the edge of the paper to avoid waste. Punch out small daisy shapes from the white paper.

2 Use a larger daisy punch to make shapes from the remaining white paper. Punch out the flower centres using a small dot or tiny flower punch and yellow paper. Punch enough shapes for about ten flowers and five leaves.

3 Use tweezers and silicone glue to create the three-dimensional effect flowers. Glue two layers of daisy shapes together, then glue the yellow centre on the top. Glue the daisies to leaf shapes if desired, then attach to the page or card.

Anna

PETER & KAY
1st Nov 1942

Alfred Buckley - My Great Grandfather

# STITCHING

Sewing or stitching on scrapbook pages is a popular technique that adds an appealing home-made touch. Hand and machine stitching can be used as a decorative feature or in the construction of a layout, such as attaching memorabilia. Almost anything can be stitched including paper, fabric, buttons and even some thin metals.

### STITCHING ON LAYOUTS

Stitching can be used as an embellishment on a page or as a way of adding dimension any existing embellishments.

Stitching itself can form a frame around a photograph or a panel of journalling. If it is used around the edges of photo mats, stitching will provide extra definition. The outside edges of a page can also be highlighted this way–blanket stitching is particularly effective.

Stitching is also utilized in the construction of a layout. Elements such as memorabilia or embellishments can be attached to the page with discreet or decorative stitches. Two layers of paper can be stitched to each other to form a pocket.

A unique background can also be created by joining together two or more pieces of paper with stitching.

### MACHINE-STITCHING

Cardstock can be sewn easily with any basic sewing machine. Just make sure to adjust the machine settings first.

Draw in stitching guidelines with a ruler and graphite pencil to help control the stitching. Carefully remove these markings when the stitching has been completed.

Experiment with different stitching techniques, such as straight, zigzag, blanket and running stitches, on your sewing machine.

A sewing machine will make stitching jobs easier, faster and provide an even appearance.

However, hand-stitching works just as well and has some advantages that a sewing machine cannot offer. A delicate layout with many embellishments will often prove too cumbersome for a sewing machine.

### HAND-STITCHING

Stitching by hand can result in either a neat or very 'handmade' finish, depending on the effect required.

If a more rustic look is wanted, consider stitching freehand to create uneven stitches in a slightly crooked line.

For a neater look with straight and even stitches the best method is to use a ruler and metal pick or large needle to pre-make the holes before stitching.

Specialized stitching placement tools, such as the 'Fiber Friend', are available. This will make the process easier as it has holes marked at regular intervals.

The wide variety of thread colours on the market makes it easier to colour-match any layout.

The best kinds of threads to use for scrapbooking projects are sewing and embroidery threads as they are archivally safe.

## HAND-STITCHING TIPS

Vary the type of thread and length of stitches to create different effects.

Create unique titles by drawing letters or patterns in pencil and stitching over the top.

Hand stitch with wire instead of thread.

Pierce thin metal shapes or metal sheets with a pick and hand-stitch them to the page.

Hand-sew buttons or other lumpy items directly onto a page.

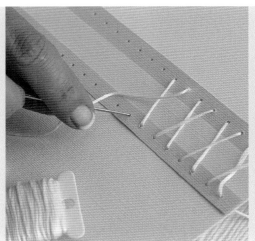

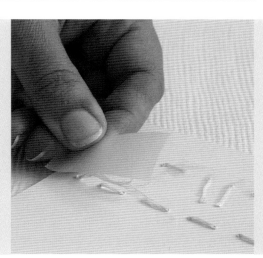

1 Using the ruler, mark the stitching points along a pencilled line, for example, about 1 cm or ¹/4 inch apart. With a pick or needle, pierce the paper at each marked interval. An easier option is to use a stitching placement tool, as shown.

2 Use tape to anchor the thread's end to the back of the paper, near the starting point of the needle holes. Pass the needle and thread in and out of the needle holes, as you would through fabric, forming the cross pattern, as shown.

3 Once the end of the row of holes is reached, anchor the end of the thread to the back of the paper with sticky tape.

# USING NOTIONS

What are notions? They are items of haberdashery that personalize scrapbook pages and add interest. Notions are not exclusive to scrapbooking and can be purchased in sewing supply and haberdashery stores. Notions can add the perfect finishing touch to a layout; choosing what to use and how to use it is all part of the fun of this hobby.

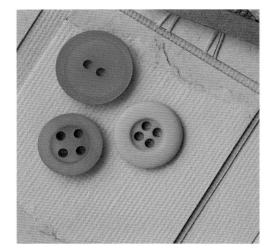

## COLLECTING NOTIONS

Sewing supply and haberdashery stores are a great source for notions, as are thrift or second-hand stores. Imaginative use of everyday items found in the home will extend your collection of notions even further.

The only limitation to using notions is that they need to be acid-free (as most fabrics are) or sprayed with an anti-acid agent.

Keen collectors of notions will check old clothes for useable parts like buttons or trimmings before throwing them out. Even the fabric itself can be used.

Notions are often handed down in the family and an old button box is a treasured find for the avid scrapbooker. Old-fashioned buttons and laces look especially lovely on heritage layouts and may themselves be a family heirloom.

## RIBBON, LACE AND THREAD

Ribbons and laces are easily acquired and have many uses. Use ribbon for a small bow to embellish a photo mat. Wrap ribbons and lace around the entire layout and tie in a bow to form a pretty border. Trim the edge of a heritage photo mat or journalling box with lace.

Small roses made from ribbon can be purchased ready-made in a rainbow of colours and they make attractive embellishments or borders.

Threads, string and twine are used to tie items to the page. They can also be wrapped around frames or small envelopes. Thread them through eyelets to form borders on layouts and photo mats or use them to hang tags.

A twisted ribbon made from your own combination of different kinds of fibres is a pretty and unique way to embellish a layout with some old-world style.

## BUTTONS AND FABRIC

Buttons are a favourite as they sit flat and can be sewn or glued to a layout.

Buttons can be used in a number of ways—as part of the title (such as a small button on top of the letter 'i'), sewn onto the corners of photos and journalling boxes, lined up to form a border or attached to a tag.

Choose fabrics for colour or texture according to the theme of the page. Use darker, rich-coloured fabrics for autumn and winter layouts, lighter pastels for spring and vibrant colours for summer.

Wrap fabric around a photo frame or use a heavily textured fabric (such as hessian) as a photo mat.

Tulle is a lightweight and effective fabric, especially evocative on wedding layouts. Lay a piece of tulle over one corner of the layout or use scraps of tulle to dress up die-cuts.

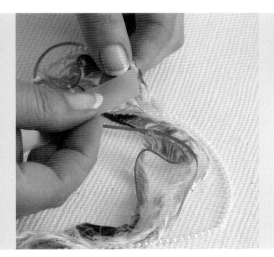

1 Select four different types of fibres of varying textures, such as pearl string, ribbons and wool. After cutting the fibres to the same length, group and secure them together by wrapping tape around one end.

2 Begin twisting or plaiting the fibres together, starting from the taped end and working down the length. When the twisting is complete, tape the unsecured ends together to prevent the twist from unravelling.

3 Attach to the front of the layout using glue dots or small amounts of silicone glue so the twist is held in place. Wrap the ends over the top and bottom edges of the layout and adhere to the back with tape or glue.

## BEADS, SEQUINS AND GLITTER

Add some sparkle to your scrapbook layouts by gluing glitter or sequins to the edges of a photo mat or journalling box. Thread beads onto wire, pins or thin thread and stitch or glue to a layout element. Beads can also be dangled on a knotted thread from the bottom of a photo mat or title.

## TWILL (COTTON TAPE)

Twill or cotton tape is used to tie items together in a bundle. Twill is very versatile as it can be dyed, stamped or imprinted, allowing you to change its colour to match the page.

Most computer printers will allow twill to be fed through easily, provided it is tightly secured to a piece of paper or cardstock. Follow the same instructions as for printing fonts on paper scraps (refer to the tips box in the section on Using Computers).

## PINS AND HOOKS AND EYES

Use pins to attach tags to frames or mats. Pins are also good for attaching photos, paper or vellum to a page. Small beads can be threaded onto a safety pin or hat. Metal charms or alphabet letters look great hanging from pins.

Hooks and eyes can also be used to hang items from a frame or mat and as connectors for fibres.

## CHARMS AND COSTUME JEWELLERY

Tiny charms, such as hearts, butterflies, flowers, keys or footballs, take on a special meaning when used on an appropriately themed page.

Charms can be tied with threads or fibres, attached with glue, threaded onto a pin or wire and attached with a jump ring or clip.

Broken jewellery or jewellery that is no longer in fashion can add a fun touch and special meaning to pages. Attach smaller jewellery items as you would attach charms.

## HINGES

Hinges come in many shapes and sizes and can be purchased from scrapbooking, hardware or craft stores. There are ornamental hinges (such as those used on jewellery box lids) or plainer, heavier hinges to choose from. They can be functional as well as decorative, and are used to create 'doors' on pages. Attach hinges with a strong silicone-based glue or crystal lacquer.

## CLOSURES (BUCKLES, D-RINGS, CLASPS)

Thread ribbon or twill through a buckle or D-ring to form a closure for a mini-book on a page. Wrap fibres around one side of the page and use a clasp to connect them at the front. Use a small buckle to join two or more ribbons around a photo mat or journalling box.

### TIPS FOR NOTIONS

Here is just a sample of the many notions used in scrapbooking.

Buttons

Threads, string and twine

Ribbons and lace

Pins (hat pins, safety pins and dressmaking pins)

Hooks and eyes

Silk flowers, dried flowers and leaves

Beads, sequins and glitter

Fabric scraps

Charms

Costume jewellery

Twill (or cotton tape)

Hinges

Closures (buckles, D-rings, clasps)

Grandma

today

smiles, laughter, squeals, ride

The          Ivy

# RUBBER STAMPING

Rubber stamping and wet embossing were around long before archival scrapbooking came on the scene. Scrapbookers now use these techniques to create distinctive backgrounds, titles and embellishments. With some knowledge and a dash of inspiration, the scrapbooker can bring a unique dimension to any layout.

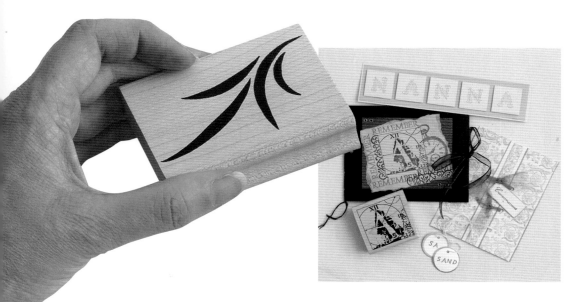

## RUBBER STAMPING AND EMBOSSING

In the past, keen 'stampers' confined their craft mainly to cards and papercraft. However, as scrapbookers are always seeking new innovations for layouts, rubber stamping and embossing are now a feature in many scrapbook albums.

The layouts in this section have all been enhanced with a rubber stamping or embossing technique. These techniques take little time, but are very effective.

Experiment with different techniques and do not be afraid to try new things. Make each layout a work of art by incorporating different media.

However, before adding rubber stamping and embossing to cherished layouts a scrapbooker must become knowledgeable about the different stamp pads and their uses.

## DYE INK PADS

Dye ink pads are water based and dry quickly on all types of paper.

These pads are acid free, permanent and sometimes waterproof, if indicated on the cover.

Dye ink pads come in a large assortment of colours. However, as the dye ink dries it becomes lighter and slightly muted.

It is recommended that scrapbookers purchase brands that are labelled archival, since archival inks are not only acid free, but fade resistant as well.

Dye ink pads are not used for wet embossing. However, they can be applied directly on paper to create a beautiful multicoloured background.

Use light-coloured dye ink pads with shadow stamps to create subtle backgrounds for titles, headings, adornments or journalling blocks.

## PIGMENT INK PADS

Pigment ink pads produce sharp and striking impressions. They provide rich, saturated colours that work well with embossing.

Pigment inks come in a wide range of colours and are acid free and fade resistant. It is recommended that clear embossing powder be used with pigment inks. However, a pigment ink can be applied without embossing as long as it is given adequate drying time.

Since pigment inks are made from particles of pigment, they work best on non-glossy paper, especially in the absence of embossing powder.

Drying time may vary, especially with metallic inks, so a heat gun may be used to set the colour. Simply hold the heat gun above the impressions and move it along in an even manner. This will help the colour set into the paper.

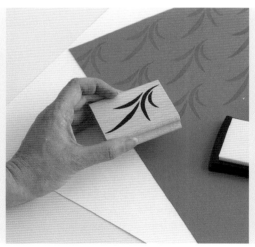

1 Choose a simple stamp to form an effective background pattern on solid green cardstock. Ink the stamp with a watermark ink pad such as VersaMark.

2 Stamp the image onto the paper. The colour of the paper will be slightly darkened, creating an eye-catching background.

3 Repeat this process until a cascading pattern is achieved. Leave the background to dry completely before assembling the layout.

## SPECIALTY INK PADS

Metallic inks are pigment inks that often require heat setting. They offer more vibrancy and pearlescence than the standard pigment pad. However, many of these pads are not child safe and some are not archival or acid free.

Recently, metallic inks that work well on all types of media and do not require heat have appeared on the market. Check labels carefully for details.

Specialty pads, such as VersaMark, provide a watermark effect on paper (see the step-by-step instructions). These create wonderful backgrounds and can be used in conjunction with chalks and Pearl Ex products.

A new product called StazOn ink can be used on a large range of surfaces like plastic, metal, glass, ceramic, laminated paper, coated paper and leather. It is a fast-drying, solvent ink that provides flexibility when creating works of art.

## EMBOSSING PADS

Embossing pads can be clear or have a slight tint that makes it easier to see an impression's placement before applying the embossing powder.

These pads are used only for wet embossing. Once applied on paper, embossing powder must be added, then heated to create a beautiful raised image.

Embossing powders come in a large assortment of colours and a few textures. Images with fine details usually require fine embossing powder for a crisp image. However, not all rubber stamps are suitable for wet embossing. Suitability is determined by the texture, grain and detail of the rubber stamps.

Often rubber stamps created from images of photographs can only be used with dye-based ink and some pigment ink pads. It is suggested that some time be spent experimenting before deciding on the best ink pad for a rubber stamp.

## EMBOSSING TOOLS

Embossing pens are an invaluable addition for any scrapbooker.

Embossing pens can be purchased in an assortment of nib styles and offer the scrapbooker the ability to emboss their own handwriting. These pens are used in conjunction with embossing powders and a heat tool.

When using wet embossing, a heat tool is the best source of heat to set the image.

The heat from a heat tool is extremely hot and, unlike a blow-dryer that blows air, it produces a direct heat that melts and sets the embossing powder.

The heat tools can be purchased in a range of styles and sizes.

Heat guns can also be used to shrink plastic that has been stamped or embossed. Read the manufacturer's directions before beginning.

## WET EMBOSSING

Wet embossing can transform an ordinary die-cut into a work of art.

In the layout Precious Little One, an ordinary blue die-cut was selected. Colour was added directly to the die-cut from a pigment-based pad. Next, clear embossing powder was applied and set with a heat tool. The process was repeated until just the right look was achieved.

The wet embossing process adds dimension to the die-cut and will naturally create a crackled effect, especially when the process is repeated a number of times.

Plain stickers can be revitalized by applying the embossing ink and then sprinkling clear embossing powder over the image. However, in this instance, the heat tool must be used with caution, since many new stickers are plastic based.

## EMBOSSING POWDERS

Embossing powders are available in a wide range of colours. They are to be used in conjunction with an embossing ink pad.

Simply ink the stamp with embossing ink and stamp the image on to the paper. Next, sprinkle on the desired embossing powder colour. Tap off the excess embossing powder. Use the heat gun to set the powder.

Once set, the image will appear raised and bolder in colour. The layout entitled Belinda shows an example of this technique. The flowers were embossed on coloured paper with white embossing powder.

Printed papers work well with the embosssing powder process and provides a more artistic feel.

## EMBOSSED PIGMENT INKS

When pigment inks are embossed they produce a beautifully raised image. The Happy Birthday layout displays this technique.

Since the layout colour was intentionally kept neutral, no further technique was applied to the image. However, once the image is embossed, chalks, coloured pencils, watercolours, and watercolour pens can be applied in order to add dimension and colour.

Using a multicoloured pigment ink pad will add an appealing gradation of colour for added interest or contrast.

# USING PENS

Pens and markers are among the most common and versatile supplies that a scrapbooker can purchase. They are made in a large assortment of nibs, colours and sizes. With some practice and imagination scrapbookers can use pens and markers to create a wide variety of lettering that will bring character to a layout.

### PEN TYPES

So many types of pens are available to scrapbookers that it is best to start off with the basic nib-styles and spend some time working with them.

The four basic nibs are monoline, chisel, scroll and brush. Many pens on the market have dual tips, one on each end. The nibs usually vary in size or style.

Since pens are permanent, create a rough draft before attempting to write on the actual layout. Draw light pencil lines on the pages to help regulate spacing and size. Once the lettering is complete and the ink has dried, rub out the guidelines with an art rubber.

Some advanced pen techniques, such as chisel pen lettering, may require extensive practice. Consider taking a beginner's calligraphy class or purchasing a step-by-step study guide available from bookstores.

### MONOLINE PENS

Monoline pens are the most commonly used among scrapbookers. They have a round tapered edge and produce a continuous line, with no deviation in thickness. The monoline pens can be purchased in a range of sizes from ultra-thin to thick. They are ideal for creating titles, borders, captions, journalling or adding embellishments.

### BRUSH NIBS

The brush nib is quite similar to an artist's paintbrush. It produces a whimsical effect that will enhance any layout. The brush nib, unlike the monoline, will vary in thickness, depending on the amount of pressure applied when writing. Try using the brush nib on its side rather than the tip. A heavier, wider stroke should be used on the downstroke, and a much lighter touch on the upstroke.

### CHISEL-TIP AND SCROLL-TIP PENS

The chisel-tip pen is slightly more difficult to use. Produce broad and narrow strokes by holding the nib at a 45-degree angle. Movement should be perpendicular to the body, keeping the pen at the same angle. Letters will be formed parallel to the sides of a page rather than with a slant or slope. The scroll-tip pen is similar but has a notch placed directly in the middle. This added feature produces a double line when writing. Use these pens to border journal entries, title boxes or captions.

### GEL PENS

Gel pens are another favourite of avid scrapbookers but only use those that are of archival quality and acid free. They come in a large assortment of colours and features, such as glitter, milky, metallic, pastel and fluorescent finishes.

## PEN TIPS

Store pens flat to prevent ink flooding to the tips.

Avoid exposing the pens to air for long periods of time as this dries out the tips, making writing less even.

Do practise pen work on scraps of actual paper from layouts so you get a good idea of colouring, bleed, etc.

As each pen nib produces a different result, try mixing a few together when creating titles, captions or journalling.

If using watercolours with pen work, use pens that are labelled 'permanent' so the pen ink will not run when wet.

Outline the shape of a letter with a monoline pen, then apply chalks or watercolours within the outline.

Gel pens can be used on both light and dark paper.

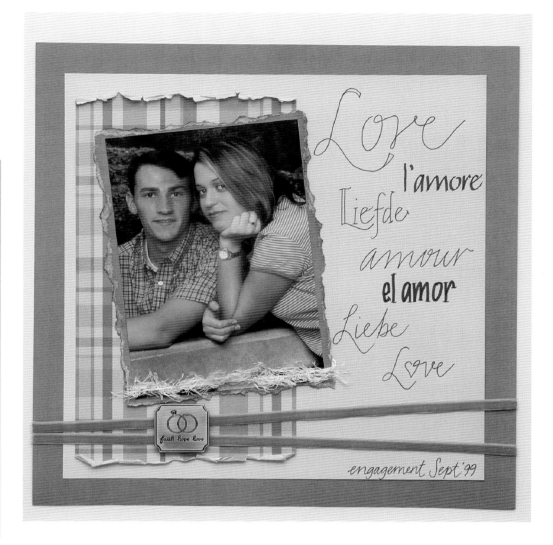

1 Select papers and prepare the layout background. Then use a soft lead pen to write the words on the paper.

2 Trace over the words with different pen nibs to create a varied look. This layout uses monoline and chisel-tip pens.

3 Erase any noticeable pencil lines with an eraser, being careful not to press too hard. Attach remaining items to complete the layout.

# CHALKING

Chalking is a technique used to give extra colour, dimension or softness to items on scrapbook layouts. It is applied effectively for an aged or distressed look, especially with heritage and 'vintage-look' designs. A small investment in a box of acid-free chalks will provide many options for decorating papers and embellishments.

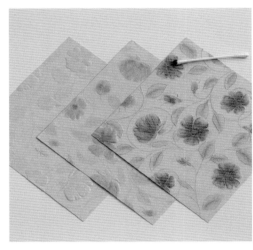

## CHALKING EQUIPMENT

An assortment of applicators will provide added flexibility when chalking. Use a cotton wool ball for large areas, or a narrow-tipped applicator for smaller areas, fine lines or edges.

Most applicators are inexpensive and can be purchased at local supermarkets. Cotton swabs or balls are good for this, as are sponge-tipped applicators (similar to eye make-up applicators). There are also special chalk applicators available which have an alligator clip to hold small cotton pompoms. Often, a small fine-tip brush will come in handy for detailed projects and when chalking embossed suede paper.

The only other tool required is an eraser to quickly repair any mistakes. A kneaded rubber eraser manufactured by Design is available at many craft or art supply stores. It will completely remove any chalk from the paper.

## APPLYING CHALKS

Always cover your work area with a large piece of paper or cloth. Choose an appropriate applicator and lightly rub it over the chalk. It is better to apply the chalk lightly and add more in layers. Using a small circular motion, lightly rub the applicator over the area to be chalked. Add more chalk to the applicator as needed, a little at a time. Continue to apply and blend layers of chalk until the desired effect is achieved.

## SEALING CHALKS

There is no need to seal chalked items with fixatives for most applications. Left alone, they will completely set within 24 hours. If a large area has been heavily chalked, turn it onto a piece of scrap paper and rub the back firmly with your hand. This will speed up the setting process by compressing the chalk into the paper fibres.

## SOFTENING EFFECTS

Whites or ivories can look too stark next to other items on a page. Try softening them with a light application of chalk to give a pale pastel finish. Lightly apply chalk to the raised edges of embossed paper to extend the colour scheme. Sand edges of patterned paper or photos to reveal some of the white paper inside, then chalk the white areas.

## AGEING EFFECTS

Age or 'distress' items using a blend of brown, grey and black chalks. Chalk the edge of torn paper for extra dimension (refer to the Vintage Collage section).

## USING STENCILS

Use stencils to apply chalked images. Dab over the open area with a chalked cotton wool ball to leave an image. Clean up untidy edges with an eraser.

## CHALKING TIPS

Choose a chalk colour one or two shades darker than the item to be chalked for definition.

Test on pieces of scrap paper until you get the right amount of colour.

Apply chalk in a circular motion for larger areas, and in a side-to-side motion for edges and thin lines.

Excess chalk or chalk dust should be tapped off the paper, rather than rubbed or flicked away.

Experiment with blending different chalk colours. Always apply lighter colours first then gradually add darker colours in layers, blending the edges with each added layer.

Add definition to the edges of chalked images with acid-free pens or pencils in co-ordinating colours.

Create negative space images by holding a cut-out shape on paper, then chalking around the edges in a light circular motion. Lift the cut-out shape up and its outline will be left on the paper, surrounded by a soft frame of chalk.

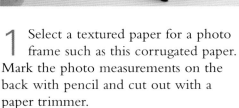

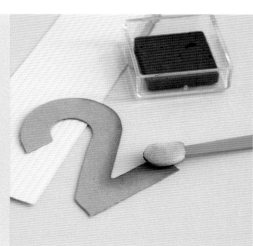

1 Select a textured paper for a photo frame such as this corrugated paper. Mark the photo measurements on the back with pencil and cut out with a paper trimmer.

2 Select a darker-coloured chalk that will blend with your layout while creating a 'three-dimensional' effect. Shade the inner and outer edge of the frame with a sponge-tip chalk applicator.

3 Use the numeral stencil or a die-cut numeral and shade the edge with the same-coloured chalk. Leave the chalked elements to set for 24 hours before attaching them to your page.

# CREATING TITLES

A title is an important element of a page. It tells the reader who the page is about or what event is being featured. It can set the mood of the page as the scrapbooker can select the colours and fonts that suit each layout. The title may be dignified and formal for a heritage or wedding layout, or hip and bright for a layout about children.

## IDEAS FOR TITLES

The inspiration for a title might be immediate or it might require some thought. Often, the inspiration can be taken from magazines, ads, cards, books, poems, quotes or song lyrics. Ideas can also be sparked by the photographs.

The title may be large and part of the focal point or it may be smaller and subtle, complementing the photographs.

Titles can be hand-drawn or created by using alphabet stickers, alphabet templates, letter tiles, stamps, alphabet beads, computer generated fonts, die-cut letters or ready-made add-ons.

The title can be embellished with coloured pencils, chalks, embossing inks and powders, beads, buttons, eyelets, brads, ribbon, raffia and other small notions.

## LETTERING STENCILS AND COMPUTERS

Lettering stencils come in a range of different fonts. To use the stencil in the Template section of this book, turn it over and trace each letter with a pencil on to the back of a sheet of paper. Cut out with a pair of scissors. This method avoids any erasing. However, some printed papers need to be face up to ensure appropriate use of the pattern. A vanishing-ink pen or a soft pencil (refer to the step-by-step section) is used when working with the stencil face up.

The computer is a fantastic tool when a quick, impressive title is needed to complete a layout. Titles can be created using computer fonts downloaded from the internet. On the Soulmate layout the title has been printed onto a piece of cardstock then hand-cut with a craft knife. A good pair of craft scissors can be used to cut titles printed onto cardstock.

## TITLE EMBELLISHMENTS

A title can be created or embellished with notions, metals and chalks to add character and appeal.

The heading 'A Day Spent with Friends' shows two different techniques. The first part was created from a computer font. The second part, 'Friends', was made by hand. Each letter was traced onto cardstock using a stencil. Depth was created by adding a darker background and embellishments (refer to the step-by-step instructions for more details).

Eye-catching titles can be created from photographs, as shown in the layout entitled Decker.

Photographs of nature-based images such as sea, sand or foliage make very effective stencilled titles.

Think twice before discarding any poor photos or cropped leftovers. Unwanted pieces can easily be transformed into special titles.

1 Remove the uppercase lettering stencil from the back of the book (see the Template section). Trace each letter onto a sheet of printed paper with a soft pencil or vanishing ink pen. Cut out with scissors and remove any pencil marks with an eraser.

2 Adhere the letter to plain cardstock to create the matting. Use a ruler or a Magic Matter disk to create the guidelines around the letter. Cut out with a scalpel or sharp pair of scissors.

3 Embellish the letter as desired. In this case, pen stroke 'stitching' was created by marking the edge of the printed paper layer with dashes to add a handmade look.

# USING METALS

Metal, in various forms, is frequently used in scrapbooking. Whether its purpose is functional or purely decorative, metal can add an element of texture or strength to a layout. Eyelets and brads have a particularly important function as they are used to attach elements, such as journal blocks or embellishments, to a layout.

## METAL ACCENTS

A wide range of metal accents and embellishments is available for scrapbooking. Metal can be used in the background, as with metal sheets and metal mesh. It can be purely decorative, as with pages embellished by small metal charms.

Text is available in the form of metal alphabets, words, plaques, bookplates, tags and tiles.

Metals frames, photo corners and hinges can be used to hold photographs. The construction of a page also makes use of metal elements such as conchos, clips and other connectors, the most common being brads (split pins) and eyelets.

Eyelets come in many shapes, sizes and colours. They can be ornamental or used to anchor elements to a layout. Fibres, wire and twine can be threaded through the eyelet holes for added texture.

## SETTING AN EYELET

To set an eyelet, you will need a hard, sturdy work surface, a cutting mat, a hole punch and hammer (the size depends on the eyelet size) and an eyelet setter.

Use a pencil to mark the spot on the cardstock for the eyelets. Pierce a hole on the mark using a hole punch that corresponds to the size of the eyelet.

Place the eyelet in the hole from the front side of the paper, then holding it in place, flip the paper over so the reverse side is up. The eyelet shaft should stick up through the hole.

Place the tip of the eyelet setter into the top of the eyelet shaft and tap the end of the setter with the hammer a few times until the edges of the eyelet shaft roll back and sit flat against the paper.

Gently tap the back of the eyelet directly once or twice with a hammer to flatten any raised areas.

## ALTERING METAL ACCENTS

All metal items can be used straight from the packet, but most can be altered to capture the distinct design of a layout. Sanding and painting are common methods of altering metals.

Sand the metal with a shiny surface before painting to help the paint adhere. Colour can then be added with acrylic paints, permanent inks or rub-ons. Sand the metal accents for a distressed effect.

Give a soft, aged look to the metal by applying white or verdigris-coloured acrylic paint over its surface, using a dry paintbrush. Do not mix water with the paint as a thicker consistency works better. When the paint is dry to the touch, use a soft cloth or paper towel and lightly rub over the edges or rub in a few spots to reveal the metal surface. This looks especially effective on metal accents with raised patterns such as decorative frames and photo corners.

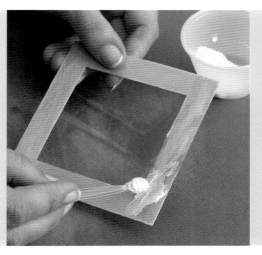

**1** Sand the metal frame with a fine-grade sandpaper to prepare the surface for proper adhesion of the paint.

**2** Prepare some thick white paint in a small cup or shallow dish without adding water. Paint the frame with a thin coat of paint using a brush or applicator.

**3** Leave the painted frame to dry overnight. For added dimension, create a dark edge around the frame with an ink pad.

# USING COMPUTERS

Computers can be one of the best resources for scrapbookers. Many font programs for scrapbookers are available on CD-ROM or can be downloaded from the internet. Scanners used in conjunction with a computer can create altered and enhanced images and are valuable for duplicating and storing precious layouts.

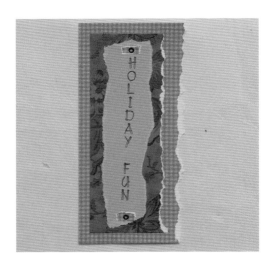  

### COMPUTER FONTS

Often scrapbookers dislike the look of their handwriting and feel that it will detract from their layouts. If this is the case, experiment with a word-processing package such as Microsoft Word.

The benefits of computer fonts are obvious—layouts look neater and more journalling will fit into allocated spaces.

Computer text can appear impersonal but this does not have to be the case. Many beautiful fonts are available, including 'hand-written fonts', that look great and match the style of any layout.

Experimenting with fonts can be fun, especially when creating vertical titles, reversed-out titles and mixing fonts within a title. The appearance of the most basic fonts already included in word-processing packages can be varied by changing the size of the letters, selecting bold and italics or varying the spacing between letters.

### FONTS FOR SCRAPBOOKS

For serious scrapbookers, special software packages (such as Lettering Delights, Creating Lettering by Creating Keepsakes, and HugWare by ProvoCraft) provide a selection of fonts and tools to add colour and pattern within the fonts.

Acquiring new fonts is easy, provided you learn about the font management system on your computer before installing the file. Most fonts come packaged in ZIP files which must be decompressed before installation.

An enormous variety of fonts can be downloaded for free from the internet. However, up-to-date virus protection is essential. Scrapbook magazines often name the fonts used in projects and this is a great way to identify attractive fonts to download. Use a good search engine, such as Google, to locate 'free font' sites, then download the desired fonts to a disk or your desktop for installation.

### SCANNING

Scanners are similar to cameras, in that they're used to capture images. They can be useful for cropping and enlarging photographs, or copying memorabilia like artworks, old packaging, old fabrics, handwriting and family heirlooms, such as jewellery.

Items such as paper clips, string or even cereal can be placed directly onto the scanner to create interesting titles.

Scanners are useful for adjusting poor-quality photos by cropping out unwanted details. Experienced computer users can improve copies of heritage photos using the scanner and computer programs such as Adobe Photoshop.

A great idea for scrapbookers is to scan albums and store them on CD-ROMs. They can be duplicated easily as gifts for family and friends. It is also a good idea to store a copy of the CD-ROM in a safe or firebox.

## FONT PRINTING TIPS

Always use acid-free computer-compatible papers. Check the printer settings (under 'media type') to achieve the best results.

Use leftover scraps of printed paper. Create a text box the same size as your scrap of paper and add journalling to fit. Print a test copy on plain paper, then temporarily attach the scrap in position with Hermafix. Run the paper through the printer, then detach your scrap.

Print the text in a light-grey colour and trace over with pens for a perfect but 'hand-done' look.

Printers vary so take time to read the instruction manual.

If printing directly on coated papers, such as vellum, allow plenty of time for the ink to dry.

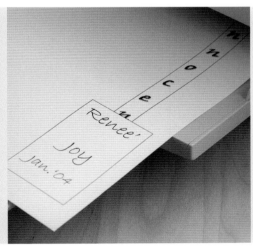

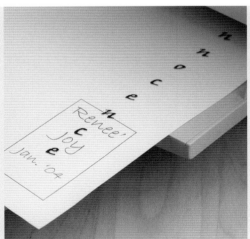

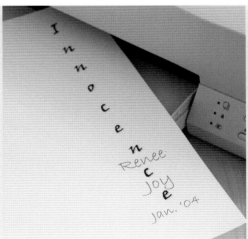

1 Insert two text boxes with appropriate measurements to fit the layout. Choose different fonts for each box. Narrow the first text box so only one letter appears on each line. If two letters appear, simply add a space. Print a test-copy on plain paper.

2 Add a shadow to the vertical text in the narrow box. Select the text box and eliminate the black outline (using the Format Text menu). For the second text box, use horizontal print that has been centred. Change the text colour to match your layout and print a test copy.

3 Ensure the two text boxes are positioned correctly. Select the second text box and eliminate the black outline. Print a test copy before printing onto cardstock (A4). If using a long piece of cardstock, make the adjustment on the page setup to reflect its actual length.

# FRAMING

Frames are not just for photos, they can be used to frame a journalling box, a title, a picture or an entire page. Frames differ from mats as they sit on top or photos, are usually wider and are often embellished. Ready-made frames can be purchased, but knowing how to make a frame to match a scrapbook theme, photograph or design is even better.

## BASIC PHOTO FRAMING

Frames can be made from specialty paper, patterned paper or almost any other material, including metal, fabric, foam core and even shrink plastic.

Consider the size of the photo when determining the width of the frame in order to maintain balance.

The frame's inside edge must be slightly smaller than the photo so that the frame completely covers the photo. The outside edge can vary in size, provided it covers the photo.

## MAKING 3-D FRAMES

Acid-free mat board is a dense, high-quality cardboard used to surround a picture with a wide mat, creating a border between it and the actual frame.

Foam core is similar to cardboard but with a foam inner medium and an outer liner of high-quality paper. Due to its thickness, a foam core frame will sit high above the photo beneath, casting a small shadow inside the cut-out area. This creates a 3-D 'shadow-box' effect that is useful for framing lumpy memorabilia.

## EMBELLISHING FRAMES

Frames can be decorated to match the colour, style and mood of a layout.

Wrap the frames in fabric, secured at the back or with ribbons tied in a bow at the front. Stitch corners for rustic flair.

Apply metallic rub-ons to a frame for a rich-looking finish. The use of heat embossing can produce a shiny enamelled finish.

Letters can be stamped onto frames or attached as cut-out letters.

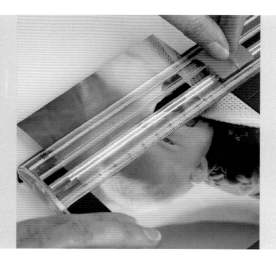 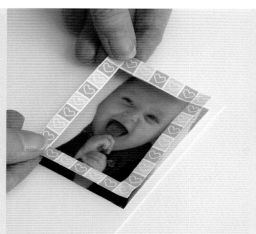 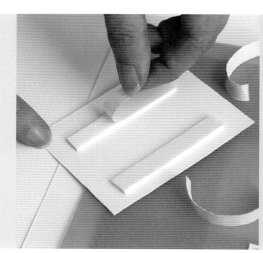

1 Push out the baby frame (see the Template section at the back of this book). Measure the frame and, if required, crop the photo with a paper trimmer. The photo will need to be slightly smaller than the outside edge of the frame.

2 Secure the photo to a mat of white cardstock with glue dots. Add glue dots to the back of the push-out baby frame and attach the frame to the photo.

3 Cut out the matted photo frame and stick two strips of Magic Mount to the back of the matting. This will create a raised picture when the matted photo is attached to the layout.

precious

...And when you finally fly away,
I'll be hoping that I served you well,
For all the wisdom of a lifetime,
No one can ever tell—
But whatever road you choose,
I'm right behind you win or lose
Forever Young...

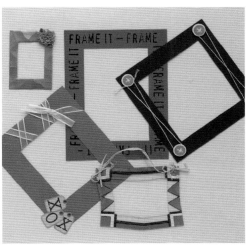

# FINDING INSPIRATION

Inspirations for innovative scrapbook layouts can be obtained from items in our everyday world. Greeting cards, magazine advertisements and wrapping papers can all spark creativity. An inspiration can steer the complete design of a layout or be used to create one or more elements to complement your page, such as titles.

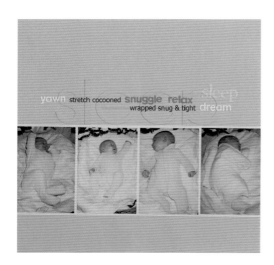

## SOURCES OF INSPIRATION

Television commercials, magazines, newspapers, the internet, billboards, books, cards, wrapping paper and gift bags can all inspire fantastic designs.

Scrapbook products can also be a source of inspiration. If a product on the market catches your attention but does not complement the photographs, create your own embellishment in colours or material that match the layout.

Surfing the internet for scrapbook techniques and ideas can be great fun. Use a search engine, such as Google, and key in the word 'scrapbooking'. An amazing number of sites will appear.

Email lists can also provide input from scrapbookers from all over the world and the inspiration to complete those hard-to-finish layouts. Send questions and receive replies over the internet, but be prepared to share your ideas as well.

## MAGAZINES

Magazines can be very helpful for scrapbookers. They provide numerous possibilities for layout designs, colour combinations and title ideas. Begin to look at magazines in a new way, especially the advertisements. They may hold the key to a winning layout. Keep a sketch book handy to outline any ideas for future reference.

The Hunter Valley and Sleep layouts were inspired by advertisements from two different magazines. Pay close attention to the fonts selected and the way space is utilized on the page.

Looking at page and advertisement designs in the latest magazines can help you to develop a very contemporary layout style.

If you are working on heritage layouts you may want to take inspiration from magazines or books of the era.

## INSPIRED JOURNALLING

Inspirations provide not only ideas for design but also the words for journalling.

Often, a greeting card might be the inspiration for a title or quote used within a journalling block. A quick scan through some old cards may inspire some great lines for future layouts or help when you can't find the right words.

Well-known phrases have a timeless appeal and song titles can also be fun to use on a layout. People's nicknames or pet names can sometimes be the inspiration for titles and often add a whimsical flavour to a layout.

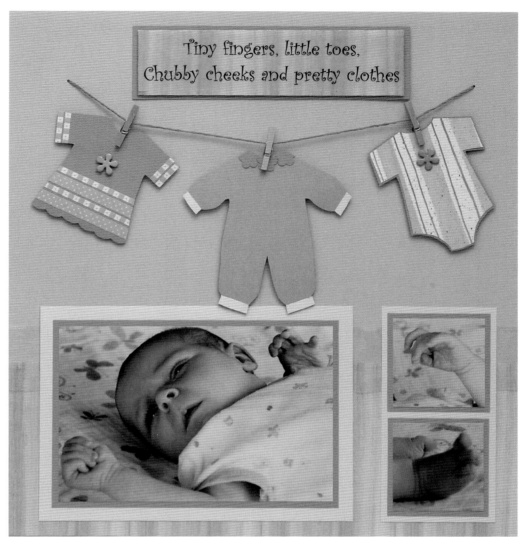

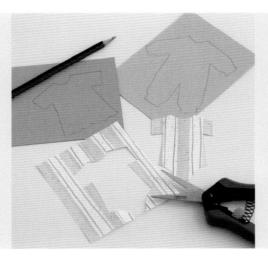

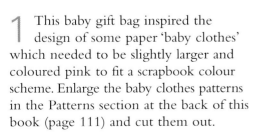

1 This baby gift bag inspired the design of some paper 'baby clothes' which needed to be slightly larger and coloured pink to fit a scrapbook colour scheme. Enlarge the baby clothes patterns in the Patterns section at the back of this book (page 111) and cut them out.

2 Place the patterns on a selection of coloured cardstock. Draw around the templates with a pencil. Cut around the outline with a sharp pair of scissors.

3 Add suitable embellishments, such as these pink eyelets and brads. Attach the cardstock clothes to the layout using tiny pegs and cord.

Emma
December '03

travel

AROUND
the WORLD

# CREATING A HERITAGE ALBUM

A heritage album is a wonderful way to preserve the past. Creating an album will involve older family members in a unique piece of historical research and provide a fascinating story for younger members of the family. As heritage photos are usually rare and precious, every effort must be taken to ensure their prolonged life for future generations.

### SORTING PHOTOGRAPHS

Before starting to scrapbook a family's heritage album, some time must be spent sorting old photos and memorabilia.

It's always a good idea to have clean hands as fingerprints will cause damage to the photographs.

Begin sorting the photographs in chronological order. If possible, make some time to sit with the oldest-living relative to gain more insight into the photograph's background.

Names of people, places and events will help when compiling the journalling. Possible dates or eras and knowing the relationship connection will bring clarity when creating the album.

This information will also provide some details that may be used to complete a search on the internet or at a local historical society.

### PHOTOGRAPH RESTORATION

While sorting the photos, you may find there are many photographs that require restoration. There are several options when restoring photographs. The most professional, and most expensive, finish is provided by a photo conservator.

Colour copiers can be used as a quick option but will not provide optimal results. Other affordable options include using duplicating machines like the Kodak Image Maker Machine, available in many chain stores. They will restore colour and make minor corrections to old photos.

It may take some time and effort, but photographs can be restored using a home computer, quality scanner and photography software. There are numerous software products available that produce professional results.

### CROPPING

It is not recommended that heritage photographs be cropped. The only time it might be appropriate to crop is when the photograph has torn edges or markings. In this case, use the paper trimmer, sparingly, to remove the unwanted areas.

A better option would be to find a frame that hides the worn areas. Framing can showcase heritage photographs, especially frames in oval shapes.

It is best that you have several copies of heritage photographs to be used for special features. These copies can then be cropped, collaged and altered to create interesting layouts.

The originals can be stored in protective acid-free pockets on the back of layouts.

For more tips on altering photographs or papers, refer to the Vintage Collage section of this book.

My Great Grandfather James Albert Cannon with his
second wife Winnie, during WWII

## HERITAGE TIPS

Use a de-acidification spray to preserve paper documents. This will not repair any past damage, but it will prevent further damage and prevent acid migration to other items on the layout.

Photocopy any newspaper clippings onto acid-free, off-white paper for a more authentic look. Chalking can also age the documents.

Colour-copy one side of a postcard, then attach the original on the page using photo corners. Place the copy next to it on the page, so both sides can be seen at once.

Collect heritage-embellishment products such as tags, frames, vintage writing, reproduced vintage postcards, postage stamps, labels and tickets to use on layouts.

## FAMILY TREES

A heritage album is relatively easy to organize and plan as the number of photographs, memorabilia and details is known prior to beginning.

A great way to start a heritage album is to complete a family tree. The family tree will display the whole family and provide the necessary connections for future reference.

Written names, small photographs or a combination of both may be used to create this type of layout. There are printed papers manufactured with family tree outlines that make the job easier. Specialized computer software programs will create beautiful family trees that can then be printed, cut out and placed on a scrapbook layout.

Use the push-out family tree frames (see the Template section at the back of this book) to create your own family tree. Reduce or enlarge family pictures so the

face of the person who is featured will fit inside the frame. This can be done with a colour photocopier or scanner, but always print onto acid-free paper.

Add glue dots to the back of the push-out frame and secure it to the copy. Write the person's name in the panel and add the framed picture to your family-tree layout.

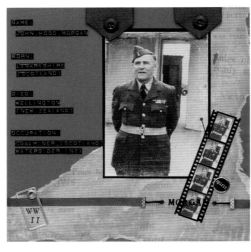

## BACKGROUNDS

Muted background colours are often preferred in heritage albums as they reflect a more vintage feel. A stylish choice is to use particular shades of colour to represent each side of the family, for example, a father's side in shades of blue and a mother's side in shades of burgundy.

## ATTACHING ITEMS

Photo corners are a great attachment option for heritage layouts as the items can still be removed if required. Photo corners can also hold memorabilia in place. Photo slit punches work in the same way. Permanent adhesives are not recommended for heritage albums.

## MEMORABILIA

Memorabilia can help families connect with the past. Some suggested items for a heritage album are handwritten recipes, old documents, such as marriage certificates, fabric from clothing, letters, pins, rings, handkerchiefs, monogrammed items, old lace and crocheted pieces.

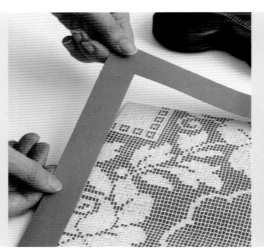

1 Select a piece of old cream-coloured lace or a handkerchief and a large sheet of dark-coloured cardstock (A3). Place under a colour photocopier, lace side down. Make copies on large, acid-free copy paper (A3). Don't worry if the lace has flaws as these will add character.

2 Create a frame 30.5 x 30.5 cm (12 x 12 inches) square and about 5 cm (2 inch) wide from matching cardstock. Position the frame over the colour copy, taking into account the features of the lace. Attach the frame with spray glue and trim the copy to fit.

3 Decorate a copy of a heritage photo using cotton lace fixed to the back with glue dots. Make several layers of matching photo mats and embellish the layout with ribbons, dried flowers and charms.

Circa 1875

# VINTAGE COLLAGE

The vintage or deliberately aged look is very popular with scrapbookers because it creates the feel of bygone eras. A wonderful range of ready-made 'shabby-look' products is available from most craft stores. However, there are many ways to achieve the aged look by using your own memorabilia and rapid-ageing techniques.

## THE VINTAGE LOOK

The vintage look is best described as scruffy and worn, but with an overall sophistication. Vintage features can range from sepia tones or rustic finishes to the rubbed-back or 'distressed' look typical of the feminine 'shabby chic' style.

Rapid-ageing techniques are particularly useful when incorporating new copies of old documents with other items that are more mellow in appearance.

The following techniques can be applied to photos, but do not use originals.

## PAPER AND CARDSTOCK

Various techniques can give paper and cardstock a worn look.

Popular methods are paper tearing, paper rolling, paper crumpling and paper scraping (refer to the relevant sections).

Paper can be sanded lightly with sandpaper or steel wool to remove some of the pattern or highlight creases.

Peel layers off the cardstock or chipboard at the corners or around the edges, leaving some layers loose and curling up to create a worn effect.

## CHALKING

Chalking is the most popular technique to age paper and cardstock.

Chalk edges after tearing, or chalk the entire piece.

Medium-brown, dark brown and black chalks give the best vintage look. Apply the chalks lightly at first, then add more as needed.

Chalking over the top of crumpled paper or cardstock will add a subtle, mellow look, especially if the creases are emphasized.

1 Mix the walnut-ink crystals with warm water until they dissolve. Test the strength on the scraps of paper you intend to use, using a small paintbrush.

2 Dip the brush in the walnut ink and lightly cover the paper to tone down the brightness.

3 Repeat the inking process if a darker colour is desired. Leave the paper to dry completely. Add extra depth with chalking and inking if desired.

## WALNUT INK

Walnut ink is made of finely ground walnut shells, and usually comes in crystal form. It is not guaranteed to be acid-free so do not use it directly on photos or allow inked items to come into contact with photos, unless sprayed with a de-acidifying product.

Walnut ink can be used in a multitude of ways. Items can be dunked directly into the ink, or ink can be applied with a soft rag, brush, scrunched-up paper towel or cotton wool ball for different effects. Walnut ink can be sprayed, spattered with a toothbrush or dropped directly on paper.

Experiment on different colours of cardstock. A light wash over pink cardstock makes a lovely antique-rose colour. Vintage fabrics and fibres can be treated with walnut ink. A strong mixture of walnut ink can also be used for writing with a calligraphy pen.

## OTHER AGEING TECHNIQUES

Rubbing edges with metallic rub-ons will give them a gilded look. An unevenly gilded item is perfect for evoking the look of faded grandeur.

Lightly smear or dab an inkpad directly onto the paper, or just to its edges. Applying ink lightly over the top of crumpled paper or cardstock adds extra depth to the overall effect.

When applied sparingly with a dry brush, acrylic paint can give a lovely worn look to patterned paper.

Embellishments can be given the shabby treatment. Sand premade items, such as buttons, wood, metals, stickers and other embellishments. Almost anything can be sanded. Apply acrylic paint to metals or plastics and then wipe off the excess before it dries. This works particularly well with paints that are white, black or verdigris coloured.

## COLLAGE

The busy, but organized, look of collage is a popular trend in scrapbooking, especially in heritage albums where its vintage appearance works well. When building a collage-style layout, ensure the design does not overpower the photos.

Larger photos stand out better from the busy background. A number of smaller photos placed in a group can look effective. Generally, one-third of the layout should consist of photographs.

Do not introduce too many colours. Collage is about a merged overall effect rather than any individual item standing out. Shapes and textures will take on extra focus. Use round shapes (such as an optical lens, round page pebble or clock face) to set off rectangular shapes. Use long, thin shapes (twine, ribbons, etc.) to connect and 'ground' items to the layout.

Mix textures by using paper, glass, plastic and metal items together.

# 1962

They were the best of times, they were the worst of times…

Nobel Prize for Physiology or Medicine: James Watson (US), Maurice Wilkins, and Francis Crick (both UK), for determining the structure of deoxyribonucleic acid (DNA)

The first transatlantic television transmission occurs via the Telstar Satellite, making worldwide television and cable networks a reality.

Lt. Col. John H Glenn is the first American to orbit Earth - three times in 4 hours 55 minutes (Feb 20).

Marilyn Monroe dies of a drug overdose at age 36.

Equality \E*qual"i*ty\, n.; pl. [L. aequalitas, fr. aequalis] The condition or quality of being equal; agreement in quantity or degree as compared; likeness in bulk, value, rank, properties, etc.; as, the equality of two bodies in length or thickness; **an equality of rights**

integration

World Population: 3.136 billion

Vatican II is convened

World Cup: Brazil 3 v Czechoslovakia 1

Song of the year: Moon River by Henri Mancini & Johnny Mercer

Best Picture: West Side Story

Best Actor: Maximilian Schell, Judgment at Nuremburg

Best Actress: Sophia Loren, Two Women

# TRAVEL

Travel photos are often accompanied by collections of related memorabilia. By scrapbooking a travel album you can make the most of your special memories. A box frame is an especially evocative method of preserving and displaying a colourful collection of travel photographs, postcards and other mementos.

### TIPS FOR TOO MANY TRAVEL PHOTOS

If there are too many photographs for one layout, consider the following suggestions:

Scan and reduce the size of some of the photos

Use expanding pages and flip pages to stretch layouts.

Construct a mini accordion-style book and secure it to the page.

Make a pocket for the extra photos.

Scan and store photographs onto a CD which can be included on a layout for easy access.

### TRAVEL PHOTOS AND MEMORABILIA

People often dedicate a whole album to a special trip or family vacation, including photos and memorabilia.

Items collected on the trip that will help in the recollection of events and places experienced throughout the journey include itinerary, tickets, boarding passes, brochures, hotel receipts, foreign currency, maps and tourist guides.

If travelling regularly, consider creating one album that features the trips in chronological order. If the trip is lengthy an entire album may be necessary to display all the pertinent photographs and memorabilia that have been collected.

Most people would organize their travel album in chronological order. Others may create their album by country, tour itinerary, or highlights of favourite places.

### TRAVEL ALBUMS

After unpacking from a trip and settling back into life, make some time to organize your photos and memorabilia. Do not wait too long to complete this task as important details connected with the items may be lost with time.

Once the sorting has been completed, start sketching each layout.

Select the photographs and papers to be used with each layout. The colour of the papers should complement the photos and can at times be selected specifically to recapture the feel of a location.

A box frame is a good way of displaying travel memorabilia. Refer to the section on Memorabilia so you know how to care for any keepsakes.

## JOURNALLING

The easiest way to remember the experiences on a trip is to keep a travel diary. Spend time each day recording the highlights and any interesting facts or phrases associated with the location. This will build the foundation for journalling later on, when the album layouts are being completed.

The information from the diary will make the journalling more meaningful as specific details can be recalled.

When journalling, ask for specific accounts or recollections from all family members. This will vary the flavour of the album and provide diverse viewpoints. Often, the younger generation see things differently and this might add a refreshing insight into the photographs.

Other things that will be fun to record are the prices of items, foods eaten and unusual local customs.

## MEMORY TRIGGERS

Postcards and photographs can assist the journalling process. Taking shots of street and city signs, monument plaques and public transport can trigger memories and help connect them in a layout.

Journalling should include any funny and amusing things that happened on the trip. Photographs are not always necessary to record these moments as the camera is usually tucked away when they occur.

Use travel guides to assist with the journalling as they provide accurate information on places, especially historical sights.

Inclusion of map sections may also help make the connection and highlight the route travelled.

Remember to spray items with a de-acidifying spray before including them in a layout.

## EXTRA IMAGES

Postcards purchased when travelling can be a great back-up for photographs. Postcards capture the images that may be missed, such as a view of the Eiffel Tower at night, aerial views of the Grand Canyon, or underwater photos of the Great Barrier Reef.

Postcards also come in handy if the photographs do not develop well. If you arrive home to find that snapshots didn't turn out as well as expected, don't despair. You can scrapbook postcards and other memorabilia, such as pamphlets.

The internet is a great place to find images of the places visited and serves as a source of information for journalling. Several photographs in the Egypt layout were downloaded from the internet, as were the hieroglyphics (pictured).

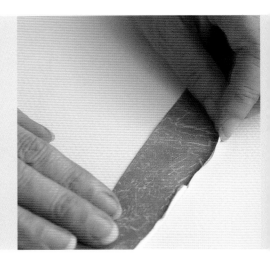

1 Select a 30.5 x 30.5 cm (12 x 12 inch) piece of cardstock to form the bottom of the box frame. Use a scalpel and cutting board to cut four pieces of foam core into strips that are 2.5 cm (1 inch) wide and 30.5 cm (12 inch) long for the sides of the frame.

2 Attach the strips to the frame with permanent adhesive squares. Trim off the excess foam core with a scalpel.

3 Cut out a frame from a 30.5 x 30.5 cm (12 x 12 inch) sheet of printed paper or cardstock. The width should be about 3.8 cm ($1^1/2$ inches). Attach this paper to the top of the foam core and roll back the inner edges. The foam core should not be visible.

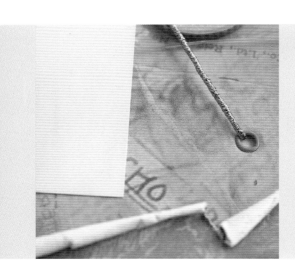

4 Use a hole punch tool, hammer and eyelet setter to set the eyelets throughout the frame bottom. Thread gold cord through to make a crisscross pattern as shown. Tape the cord ends to the back of the page. Add a backing of plain cardstock to hide the cord ends.

5 Form a collage of photos and memorabilia. Attach these with spray glue to the frame bottom, underneath the gold cord. Memorabilia can be sprayed with 'Archival Mist' if desired.

6 Embellish the outer frame with an assortment of travel stickers. Glue stickers to photo mats made from hessian for a handmade look. Use brads and string to emphasize the three-dimensional look.

# BABIES

One of the most special scrapbooks is a baby album. It records new life entering the world and provides a pictorial account of a baby's first few years. An album offers a means of protecting and displaying treasured photographs and baby memorabilia. The actual compilation of a baby album can be a joyful and rewarding experience in itself.

### BABY PHOTOS

Photographs taken at the same time each month will show the baby's growth. Birthdays and holidays also provide special milestones.

Highlight key moments in a baby's life like the first tooth, first table food, first haircut, first-time crawling, first steps and first birthday.

Take close-ups of a baby's face, hands and feet as these features will change so quickly and the images can be very effective in a scrapbook layout.

### PAPERS AND EMBELLISHMENTS

Many beautiful printed papers and stickers are designed specifically for babies. They are predominantly soft pastels and reflect baby themes such as nursery-rhyme characters.

Embellishments featuring baby clothes and items such as bottles, bibs and nappies can be purchased or easily made. Decorate baby pages with pastel-coloured and gingham ribbon. Buttons help add shape and contrast to a layout.

### WHAT TO KEEP

Keep a journal to record the changes that occur each month, including the first time a mother feels the baby move.

Clear pockets can be added to the album to hold memorabilia. Collect ultrasound photographs, baby-shower invitations, hospital ID bracelets, name tags and congratulatory cards.

Once the baby is home, keep special items like the first bib, little booties, a lock of hair, small toys, teething rings and nappy pins.

1 Select the ribbon and cut it into four sections a little longer than double its width.

2 Fold both ends of the ribbon toward the centre, forming a right angle. Protect with a cloth such as a tea towel, then lightly press the ribbon corner with a warm iron.

3 Hold the ribbon corner in place by adding an acid-free adhesive and then securing the corner to the layout.

Emma
December '03

# WEDDINGS

The style of a wedding album depends on the type of wedding: formal, semi-formal, casual, large, small or intimate. The album should reflect the style and feel of the wedding and provide a way of reliving the experience. Select an album cover that will complement the overall presentation of this very special event.

## PHOTO SELECTION

Sort through all the photos, combining professional snaps with those taken by friends. Keep the professional photos intact and try to limit photo cropping.

Decide on a theme for each layout, such as Getting Ready, Bride and Family, Guests and the Reception. Be selective with photos. Each layout should have a focal point—one photo that captures the moment expressed by the overall layout. Surround the focal point with photos that help to support the story.

## COLOUR THEMES

As most of the photographs have been taken on the same day, one background colour can be selected to appear throughout the whole album.

Other papers and embellishments could be used from the same colour family or in complementary colours that may bring greater depth to the photographs. Decoration should be sophisticated, subtle and help to complete the layout. Create titles from elegant fonts printed onto matching-coloured papers.

## JOURNALLING

Journalling can include how you met, where and how the proposal occurred and the engagement party.

It's important to cover the lead-up to the wedding and some acknowledgement of the stresses of organizing a wedding!

Readers will also appreciate some background on participants such as attendants, witnesses and parents, and their thoughts as well. Lastly, try to recapture and express your feelings on this special day.

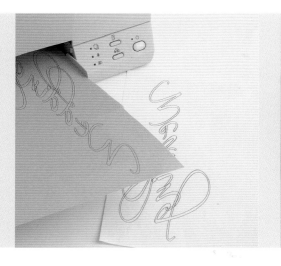  

1 Create a title in a text box sized to fit your layout. Style in an appropriate font, such as Scriptina. Format the text so it is reversed (this can be done in Microsoft Word using WordArt). Make a test-copy on plain paper, then print on the actual cardstock.

2 Cut out the heading carefully, using a sharp pair of scissors, nail scissors or a scalpel. Use the printed outline as a guide; it will not be visible when the letter is flipped over.

3 Cover the side of the letter that shows the outline with a repositionable adhesive such as Hermafix. Flip the letter over and fix it to the page. Check the original text to determine the spacing between the letters.

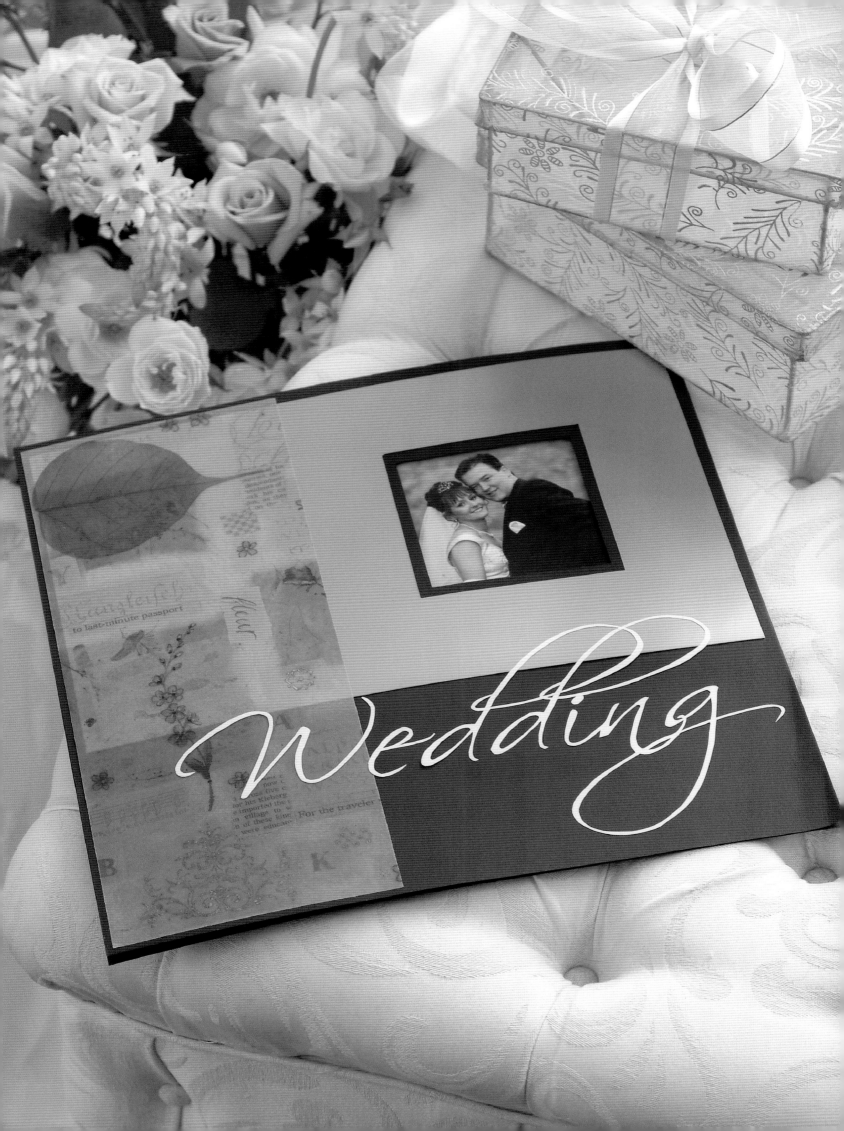

# HOME AND GARDEN

Keen scrapbookers develop the habit of scrapbooking everything about their world, such as home life, renovations and the garden. Remember that even seemingly mundane details may interest children or grandchildren in the future. Scrapbooking a garden diary will also provide an attractive guide to planting that the homeowner can use in years to come.

## PHOTOGRAPHING THE HOME

A great way to relive a childhood is to visit the home in which you were raised. If the home is still inhabited by parents or other relatives, then it would be possible to photograph the inside as well as the outside of the house.

To help capture all the memories of a home, take photographs of its main features: the front door; the letterbox; the clothesline; and favourite areas. Try to take photographs at different angles, especially of the architecture.

Focus on everything that makes up the home, such as furniture, knick-knacks, curtains or blinds, pictures, plants and any structural highlights such as wooden beams.

If a home is being bought or sold, take fun photographs of the entire family standing in front of the 'For Sale' or 'Sold' signs.

## THE HOME ALBUM

Select colours for the layouts that are reminiscent of the particular room or location featured in the photographs. Use fabric from lounge suites, paint from walls and tiles from the kitchen as inspiration for colour choices. Adding fabric and paint swatches in a layout will bring connection and texture to the overall presentation.

When journalling, mention personal details such as why the home is endearing or special to the family, and, if moving, include reasons for this decision.

Mention people such as the neighbours, distances to schools, local shops, parks, work and favourite neighbourhood places. Include a map of the local area somewhere in the album. This will help future generations understand the journalling, especially when referring to schools, local shops or special features in the community.

## RENOVATIONS

A common theme in home scrapbooks is renovations. Major home renovations usually represent a considerable personal achievement and investment of time and money. A record of the process will be both emotionally satisfying and useful for showing others.

An effective approach is to simply scrapbook layouts that show before and after photographs.

In the journalling, discuss the time it took to complete, the costs incurred, plans for the renovations and plans for the future.

Local scrapbook stores sell a large range of embellishments that can be used effectively on layouts about the home. Recently, some product lines have based their colour schemes on paint chips used for interior decorating. Using a core colour palette simplifies the process while creating a stunning result.

## THE GARDEN

The garden is an integral part of the home. Throughout the years, a garden evolves along with the tastes of its caretakers. Photographs, sketches and plant samples can capture the garden's development and can be enjoyed for years to come.

Because of the transient nature of the garden it pays to keep a month-by-month diary with a photographic record of any garden triumphs.

Prized flowers can even be preserved in a scrapbook if they are suitable for pressing.

Create garden planners that record what you planted and where. In time, this will indicate which plants flourish best in the garden and where plants like spring bulbs are due to appear next season.

Garden plans can also help in the future for remembering the name of a rose variety or the year a tree was planted.

## WHAT TO KEEP

Gardeners often need to keep scraps of information related to their garden, such as plant tags or the growing instructions on a seed packet. These can rapidly accumulate into an untidy mess.

Clean important seed packets or plant tags carefully. Spray them with archival mist to protect any photos included in the layout. Seed packets can also be scanned and printed if you have the equipment.

Preserved flowers, seeds and leaves were featured in scrapbooks during the Victorian era. Old-fashioned methods of flower preservation still work, such as hang-drying flowers or pressing petals in a book or press.

However, flowers for the scrapbook can now be preserved by using a microwave oven (see the step-by-step instructions) and they can also be laminated with a Xyron machine for extra protection.

## DESIGNING GARDEN LAYOUTS

Garden layouts are fun to design and can reflect different gardening styles such as colourful and slightly messy or geometric and orderly.

Shadow-box frames are a great way to protect small items of memorabilia (refer to the Garden Diary layout). Use foam core cut out with a scalpel knife to create the raised frame.

An interesting 'window frame' effect (shown in the Spring layout) can be created by photo cropping. Mark a grid pattern on the back of the photograph with a ruler and graphite pencil. Cut along the grid lines with a sharp pair of scissors. Alternatively, make the sections with a square-hole punch.

When sticking the photo pieces to the page, leave an even gap between each piece to make a 'mosaic' design. Do not try this with one-of-a-kind photos.

## GARDEN TIPS

These items make wonderful inclusions in a garden scrapbook:

Lightweight garden markers

Scanned or cleaned seed packets

Dried, pressed flowers

Dried seeds and skeleton leaves

Original garden plans

Cuttings from plant catalogues and newspaper or magazine articles

Clear, raised page pebbles (used in the Garden Diary layout)

Mosaic-style 'windows'

Raised frames

Floral fabrics

Twine

Garden template pictures

1 Select well-formed petals or small whole flowers. Wrap the petals or flowers in tissues and place inside a flower press.

2 Place the press (metal press screws must be removed) inside a microwave oven. Weigh down with microwaveable plates. Microwave on high for 20 seconds. Times will vary, depending on the moisture content of the flower.

3 Allow to dry completely before attaching the petals to the layout with a small amount of acid-free craft glue. Petals can also be sealed with craft glue or laminated with a Xyron machine for extra protection.

# MINI ALBUMS

Mini albums and books can be quick to create and make great gifts or keepsakes. Use them to experiment with new techniques or styles. Mini albums are a good starting point for a new scrapbooker as a whole album can be completed in just a day or two. These albums come in a variety of sizes and shapes, including popular tag books.

## ALBUM SHAPES AND SIZES

Premade blank mini albums and books can be purchased from scrapbook stores, ready to be filled with photos and embellishments. These are a good option if time is an issue.

However, the actual construction of a mini album or book is easy, and offers additional options for embellishment before binding the pages together.

There are a few considerations to keep in mind before assembling a mini album or book. Choose a shape that will work best with the theme and the selected photographs; options include square, rectangular or tag shapes.

Tag books make especially good gifts. To make a tag book similar to the one used for 'Travel', follow the step-by-step instructions provided.

## MINI-ALBUM THEMES

Almost any theme is suitable for a mini album. Baby brag books are perfect to keep in a handbag to show off those special baby snaps, or as a gift for a grandparent. Family albums with photos of family members through the years can become treasured keepsakes.

Travel albums with photos, memorabilia and journalling are a quick reminder of a favourite trip.

Wedding albums can show a selection of some of the best photos from a wedding. This makes a wonderful gift for those important anniversaries.

A yearbook is a small pictorial diary of a year in your life. Include everyday photos as well as any special events.

Inspirational albums are a collection of your favourite poetry and quotes. Include some empty pages at the back for future use.

The '10 reasons why' albums are a perfect pocket-sized gift for special occasions such as Mother's or Father's Day (10 reasons why you are the world's best dad or mum); Valentine's Day (10 reasons why I love you); or a friend's birthday (10 reasons why you're my best friend).

Children's personalized storybooks are ideal for the mini-album format. Make up a short story that includes your child and add pictures that go with it. Cut out pictures from old books or magazines, or download them from the internet and print them onto white cardstock. Children love these!

Decide on your theme, then plan the pages in advance so adequate amounts are created. For example, if making a year-in-review album, you may want to allow two pages for each month—one for photos and one for journalling.

## COVERS

The mini album can be either hard-covered or soft-covered.

Hard covers are made using chipboard or mat board and are recommended for albums that will be frequently used, such as brag books.

Soft covers are made with cardstock and are perfectly adequate for albums or books that are attached to pages, or not used frequently.

## BINDING

Pages can be stitched, stapled or glued together. You can also connect hole-punched pages with hinged rings, twine or waxed linen. Office supply stores also sell a variety of binding systems.

For a really special album, consider having it professionally bound by a printing company that offers this service.

## CLOSURES

Mini albums can have a closure at the front or the side. For smaller accordion-style albums that are to be included on a page, closures aren't necessary as the page protector will stop them flying open.

Tag books are usually left without a closure, as they tend to lie or stand reasonably flat.

For larger mini albums some form of closure may be wanted—either for functional or decorative purposes.

Some closures can be complicated, but there are three quick and easy methods. Wrap a length of cotton tape around the album and use a buckle or D-ring to hold the ends together.

Tie ribbon or twine around the album and join it in a bow at the front.

Feed a ribbon through eyelets placed on the edge of the front and back pages and tie it in a bow.

## OTHER IDEAS FOR MINI ALBUMS

Mini albums don't have to be stand-alone albums. Very small albums can even be attached to the pages of standard 30.5 x 30.5 cm (12 x 12 inch) albums.

These smaller albums can, for example, hold additional photos that wouldn't otherwise fit on the layout.

If a very small album is to be included on a layout, make sure there is enough room left on the page to attach it, and decide how this will be accomplished.

If it is not too heavy, simply attach the back page of the small album to the scrapbook page with glue.

These small albums can be connected to a layout with threads or ribbon. Punch holes in the layout and feed ribbons through the holes. The ribbons can then be tied to the smaller album.

1 Purchase about 6 to 10 large tags for the actual book pages, and a few smaller tags for layering. Or, make your own tags from cardstock. Choose stamps, papers and stickers that will enhance the selected theme. Stamp a background onto a large tag using a brown dye-based ink pad.

2 Decorate the smaller tags with stamps, photos, and torn journalling. Add dimension and shading by applying chalks in various shades of brown and a touch of black around the edges for definition. Set the small tags aside.

3 Embellish the large tag by alternating layers of torn printed papers and stickers. Torn edges can be chalked for subtle blending. Do not include any bulky items near the left edge as eyelets will be added for assembling the tags into the book.

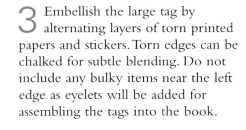

4 Attach the smaller tag to the larger tag using double-sided adhesive foam. Align all the premade holes with each other. Position this tag over another and poke a pencil through the eyelets to mark a dot on the tag below. This will ensure proper placement of eyelets on each tag.

5 Attach the eyelets to each of the remaining tags where the pencil marks have been made. Attach eyelets to the cover for extra reinforcement. Remaining stickers may be added to the inside covers for continuity and visual appeal.

6 Slide the tags in the correct order (from last page to first) onto two hinged rings fed through the eyelets. Snap the hinged rings closed. Select matching ribbons or fibres to insert through each tag as shown.

# THEMED ALBUMS

A themed album focuses on one idea or subject throughout its pages. Themed albums make unique, wonderful presents that can be frequently revisited and are unsurpassed by commercial items. The homemade look adds an endearing personal quality. The creation of a matching cover is the finishing touch to this one-of-a-kind gift.

## SPECIAL THEMES

A well-chosen and presented themed album is a great way to commemorate special occasions or relationships with other people. Popular scrapbook album themes include family, holidays, pets, home renovations, courtships, weddings, sports and hobbies.

A themed album can be created for a birthday or anniversary present. It can be given as a thank-you or in remembrance of a special event, even to help a friend or family member through a difficult time, such as the loss of a loved one.

## COVERS

A customized cover is especially appropriate if you are creating a themed album that is intended to be a gift.

Covers that reflect the subjects or themes inside work best, but they don't have to be elaborate. A simple card or motif, even a duplication of one of the internal-page embellishments will work fabulously.

Covers can be decorated with paper or fabric. If the album is subject to frequent handling, add a protective cover made from acid-free plastic.

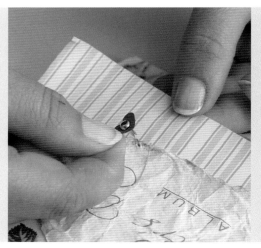

1  Select sheets of extra-thick cardstock to create the album and cover pages. Use background papers and borders that carry your theme through the book. Attach these to the cover.

2  Write or print the album title on co-ordinating cardstock. Embellish with crumpling and chalking techniques. Attach the title to the cover with heart-shaped die-cuts and small brads.

3  When all the pages are completed, punch holes through the left-hand border. Eyelets can be added for extra reinforcement. Tie the album together with co-ordinating ribbons and tassels.

## CO-ORDINATING LAYOUTS

Simplicity is the key feature of a themed album and this can easily be accomplished by using the same colours, papers or product range on every layout.

This technique will save valuable time when completing each layout, as many of the design choices in creating a layout are all pre-determined.

The overall layouts can be kept simple, uncluttered, yet effective.

Some co-ordinating embellishments can be used throughout the album to add a personal touch or further emphasize the theme. Examples of embellishments include the small heart-shaped die-cuts added to the brads on the Mother's Day album cover (shown on the previous page).

## JOURNALLING

There are many ways to structure the layouts for a themed album. The easiest way is to cover different events as they happened chronologically. However, many other options can be explored with pleasing results.

Creating layouts based on different viewpoints is an entertaining yet personal approach; for example, a Mother's Day album could be based on what a mum means to each of her children.

For a sophisticated, contemporary approach minimal journalling will draw more attention to the design and the photographs.

## PHOTOGRAPHS

Photographs from personal collections and hobbies can form the basis of a classic themed album.

The layouts on these pages were created using a collection of photos from a photographer's portfolio.

The photos tell the story so effectively that little or no journalling is required. The overall design of the layouts enhances the photographs by keeping them as the central focus.

The placement of the photographs mimics the design of the paper.

Embellishments capture an element from the photographs, as seen in the layout, 'Bad to the Axle'.

This album is a great example of less is more.

"Bad to the Axle"

# ABOUT ME!

Most family photographers find themselves behind the lens so often that they forget to make an appearance in their own albums. Scrapbookers also need to be reminded that besides photographing, journalling and embellishing the experiences of other people they should have some 'about me' space too.

## ABOUT ME TIPS

Things to include in your album:

Everything and anything to do with You

Likes and dislikes, beliefs and values

You as a child, a teen, adult, parent, partner, etc.

Childhood, including school, friends, toys and pastimes

Career, including past and current jobs, workmates, bosses, income and future career goals

## ABOUT YOU

An 'about me' album is an album based solely on the individual who creates it. It should encapsulate items from the past, plans for the future and hopes and dreams. The photographs should range from childhood to the present and include significant people in your life.

A great reason for creating an 'about me' album is to leave a legacy that will be read and cherished for generations to come.

## JOURNALLING

'About me' albums can be completed in stages; however, it helps to keep a diary and record of any important details and emotions as they happen.

Use 'backwards journalling' as a starting point for a layout. Decide what to say first, then find photos or memorabilia that support the point.

Shy journallers can make use of hidden journalling devices such as envelopes, tags, lift-up flaps, small booklets, or a CD included on the layout.

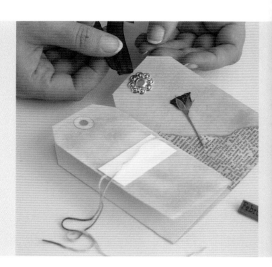

1 Select an accordion-style 'gang' tag. Write your journalling on the inside pages of the tag.

2 Chalk both sides using medium-brown and red chalks. Add some mini-photos if desired.

3 Decorate the front cover and attach string to the back page for a tie-closure (the back page will be hidden as it is fixed to the layout).

# SCRAPBOOKING FOR KIDS

Kids not only enjoy looking through completed scrapbooks but love participating too. Children as young as four years old have the ability to complete scrapbook layouts about their daily life. Scrapbooking together can be an illuminating experience as you glimpse the world from a child's perspective.

## WHEN TO BEGIN

The great thing about scrapbooking is that every member of the family can participate. Basic motor skills, especially cutting and pasting, are the foundation.

If a child shows a genuine interest in the craft, try to invest some time with him or her. Demonstrate the correct way to use the tools and discuss some basic design principles. Provide some practice and, above all, let the child be free to try new things. The end product may not be appealing at first but, with time and practice, the quality will improve.

## EQUIPMENT

Purchase a small selection of age-appropriate tools and supplies, such as a small paper trimmer, a few decorative (child-friendly) scissors, easy-to-use adhesive, coloured gel pens and stickers, including letters.

The push-out templates in this book are a very useful resource for the kids.

Save leftovers scraps from past layouts for the kids to use. It will minimize costs and provide them with a wide choice of papers. They will also enjoy using the same papers seen in other albums.

## WHAT TO INCLUDE

Include a child's writing, paintings and drawings in their scrapbook album, but do use a de-acidification spray on any non-acid-free papers. Photos of very bulky artwork are an effective substitute.

Older children may want to try their own photography and a disposable camera is a great way to start them off.

Creating an ABC album will help teach the alphabet and extend vocabulary. Older children love creating ABC albums for younger siblings and this type of album is a potential family heirloom.

1 Use the stencil template in the back of this book. Flip it over and trace each letter shape on to a piece of felt with a felt-tip pen.

2 Cut the letter out with a sharp pair of scissors. As the pen marks are on the reverse side of the felt they will not show when the letter is glued to the matting.

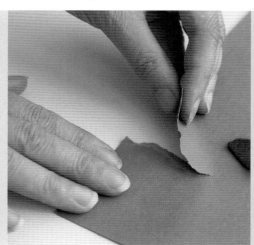

3 Use craft glue to stick the letter to matting made from torn cardstock. Set up an ABC album with one letter of the alphabet on each page. Get the kids to scrapbook any words, stickers, photos or drawings that start with that letter.

# LEFTOVER SCRAPS

As beautiful and creative layouts begin to fill a scrapbook a large collection of leftover papers and notions will begin to accumulate. Scrapbookers are naturally inventive in using up leftover scraps. Cast-off items can be transformed into stunning creations, either for a scrapbook or for other uses.

## ORGANIZING SCRAPS

The most important element when conserving is organization. Like other scrapbook supplies, the leftovers are best separated into solids and patterns, then arranged in colour groupings.

Small, clear, expanding folders work well for this and can be purchased at scrapbook or office supply stores.

Remember to use only acid-free storage components and store them in a cool, dry location away from direct sunlight.

## EMBELLISHMENTS

Notions and other embellishments can be kept in one location to prevent them from getting lost or forgotten.

Sometimes, spotting a collection of notions in a storage tray will spark off ideas for future creations.

New embellishments for a layout can easily be made with leftovers. They can be torn, aged, rolled, punched, stamped, embossed, printed and combined to create the right accent for any project.

## LEFTOVER CREATIONS

Leftover materials can be used to make beautiful cards, bookmarks, CD-holders, mini-books, placecards, journalling blocks, frames, collages and paper-piecing projects.

Just as quilters use fabric scraps to create a masterpiece, paper quilts can be created for a beautiful background on any scrapbook layout.

Utilizing the leftovers will help make the best use of a scrapbooker's investment and keep the spirit of innovation alive.

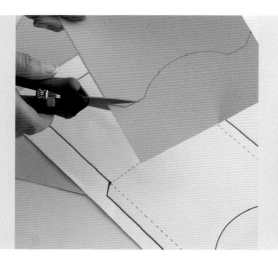

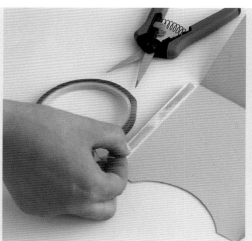

1 Enlarge the CD-cover pattern in the Patterns section of this book (page 111) on a photocopier by 200%. Trace the pattern onto a piece of leftover plain cardstock. Cut out the cardstock along the solid lines.

2 Score along the dotted lines on the cardstock, then fold the flaps inwards. Fix the sides of the CD cover together with double-sided tape.

3 Decorate the CD cover as desired using leftover scraps and embellishments. For this cover the scraps were torn and fastened with brads and eyelets.

# PROJECT MAKERS

# PATTERNS

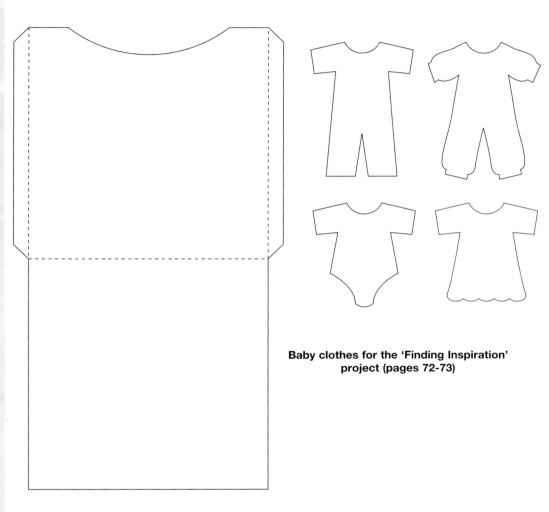

**Baby clothes for the 'Finding Inspiration'
project (pages 72-73)**

**CD Cover for the 'Leftover Scraps' project
(pages 108-109)**

**Enlarge these patterns on a photocopier by 200%.**
**Note that solid continuous lines are cutting lines and dotted lines are fold lines.**

Published in 2004 by Bay Books, an imprint of Murdoch Books Pty Limited.

© Text, photography, design and illustrations Murdoch Books Pty Ltd 2004.

**Editorial Project Manager:** Catherine Etteridge
**Designer:** Nicola Hardcastle
**Photographer:** Ian Hofstetter
**Stylist:** Anne-Maree Unwin
**Authors:** Louise Riddell, Scrapbook Cottage; Frank Saraco
**Additional Text:** Joanne Green; Leanne Hand
**Scrapbooking Consultants:** Joanne Green; Leanne Hand; Louise Riddell; Frank Saraco
**Template Design and Illustration:** Spatchurst
**Additional Illustration:** Tricia Oktober; Tracy Loughlin; Isn't She Clever Design and Illustration
**Production:** Monika Vidovic

ISBN 1 74045 380 8

Printed through Phoenix Offset. PRINTED IN CHINA.
First printed in 2004. Reprinted in 2005.

**Acknowledgements**
The publisher would like to thank the following for supplying products for photography:
Scrapbook Cottage: www.scrapbookcottage.com.au